CONNECTING NON FULL-TIME FACULTY TO INSTITUTIONAL MISSION

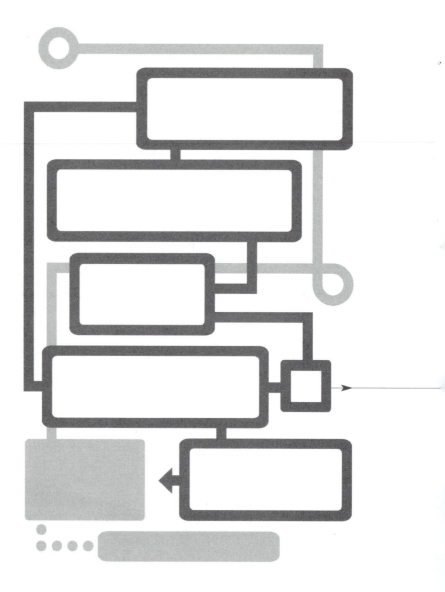

CONNECTING NON FULL-TIME FACULTY TO INSTITUTIONAL MISSION

A Guidebook for College/University Administrators and Faculty Developers

Leora Baron-Nixon

Foreword by Irene W. D. Hecht

Sty/us

STERLING, VIRGINIA

Sty/us

COPYRIGHT © 2007 BY STYLUS PUBLISHING, LLC.

Published by Stylus Publishing, LLC
22883 Quicksilver Drive
Sterling, Virginia 20166-2102

Library of Congress Cataloging-in-Publication-Data
Baron, Leora, 1943–
    Connecting non full-time faculty to institutional
mission : a guidebook for college/university administrators
and faculty developers / Leora Baron.—1st ed.
        p.   cm.
    Includes bibliographical references.
    ISBN 1-57922-060-6 (hardcover : alk. paper)—
    ISBN 1-57922-061-4 (pbk. : alk. paper)
        1. College teachers, Part-time—United States.   I. Title.
LB2331.72.B37   2007
378.1′2—dc22

                                                        2006025581

ISBN: 1-57922-060-6 (cloth) / 13-digit ISBN: 978-1-57922-060-0
ISBN: 1-57922-061-4 (paper) / 13-digit ISBN: 978-1-57922-061-7

Printed in the United States of America

All first editions printed on acid free paper
that meets the American National Standards Institute
Z39-48 Standard.

> Bulk Purchases
>
> Quantity discounts are available for use in workshops
> and for staff development.
> Call 1-800-232-0223

First Edition, 2007

10   9   8   7   6   5   4   3   2   1

For the many thoughtful individuals—part-time faculty, full-time faculty, and administrators at Florida International University and at the University of Nevada, Las Vegas, whose insights, experiences, and friendship made possible experimentation with the ideas and programs reflected in this volume.

L.B.

CONTENTS

FOREWORD

C olleges and universities have made use of adjunct faculty for years. However, both their numbers and the work they do are in the process of drastic change. In the past, adjuncts were used for one-year sabbatical appointments or in clinical and/or applied disciplines. Their appointments were distinctly either temporary or episodic.

Today there is a new reality. According to Department of Education Statistics quoted by Baron-Nixon (p. 3), by 1998, 43 percent of faculty nationally were serving on nontenurable contracts. These appointments, while not evenly distributed, are found in all varieties of institution and across all disciplines.

The publication of Leora Baron-Nixon's *Connecting Non Full-time Faculty to Institutional Mission* could not be more timely. Having sketched a portrait of the current reality of nontraditional, nontenured appointments, Baron-Nixon proceeds to the next step, namely, addressing how institutions need to adjust to the new reality. Reflections on the matter to date have tended to be laments or indictments of institutions for using these appointments largely for fiscal protection. Baron-Nixon recognizes that the reasons for using nontenurable appointments are idiosyncratic; the titles assigned are varied; the contractual definitions individualized. The variations are being created both by the needs of the faculty in question and the goals of the institutions or even departments in which they are employed. However, Baron-Nixon's ultimate message is that these nontenurable appointments are here to stay and that they are sufficiently widespread to require the creation of a new mind-set, appropriate institutional policies, and departmental interventions.

The theme Baron-Nixon has chosen is that of *connections*. Students do not differentiate between their part-time instructors and those that are full time. The hazard posed by part-time nontenurable appointments is that while students regard faculty as "faculty" and rely upon them for guidance and information about the department, discipline, and institution, nontraditional appointees may not have the requisite knowledge. Hired for their particular expertise or for defined short spans of time, such appointees, unless tutored by their departments, may know little about the requirements of the department/institution and may be oblivious to the values and purposes of the institution in which they are teaching. Ultimately, such ignorance can undermine the standards of both the department and the institution.

Baron-Nixon suggests that the new reality needs to be addressed at two levels. The first is that of institutional policy; the second is that of departmental interventions designed to connect nontraditional faculty to the department and institution.

The value of Baron-Nixon's work is that she addresses both the mundane and the conceptual. She offers suggestions for institutional policies to build uniformity of the use of titles and compensation systems at the macro level. At the micro level she speaks to the need for departments to consider the mundane matters of office space, telephone and e-mail access, and library cards and also the conceptual issues of assisting nontraditional faculty in improving their teaching and participating in professional development. In addition, she raises important issues concerning participation in departmental or even faculty governance. This may be a painful subject, but depending upon the prevalence of nontraditional appointments, it is an issue that institutions and departments need to address.

This may well be one of the first efforts at comprehensively addressing this important topic. For any institution or department ready now to look systematically at the issues of nontraditional appointments, Baron-Nixon has provided a road map that both charts the questions and points out the path toward solutions.

Irene W. D. Hecht
Director, Department Leadership Programs
American Council on Education

INTRODUCTION

The use of part-time faculty (see Connection 1, What's in a Name?) in higher education institutions can no longer be aptly termed a phenomenon. It is reasonable to assume that after almost four decades of consistent growth to a high of approximately 46 percent of all faculty, part-time faculty are a permanent and important part of teaching and learning at community, junior, and vocational colleges, four-year colleges, and universities. It is, therefore, counterproductive not to deal with issues related to part-time faculty employment due to limited financial conditions or shortsighted political conditions, nor is it prudent to ignore the issues for fear of resistance to change, or because everyone will get used to the status quo.

This volume is rooted in several key assumptions:

1. Institutions want to provide the best possible education to their students.
2. Institutions want to encourage and maintain the highest level of professionalism among their faculty.
3. Institutions want to foster and to show appreciation for a culture of quality.
4. Institutions want to maintain a collegial community of teachers and learners.
5. Institutions want to be an integral part and a respected member of the communities in which they exist.

Regardless of each institution's financial and political realities, when all is said and done, institutional growth and continued success depend, to a large extent, on "doing it right" when it comes to working with part-time faculty. The political and financial implications of not treating part-time faculty in an equitable and professional manner, while they may vary from place to place, ultimately may prove costlier. Due to their numbers and sphere of influence (i.e., basic, core, and specialized professional courses), part-time faculty possess real potential to influence the quality of education locally and nationally.

Most of the suggestions here are highly cost effective in that they involve changed attitudes and relationships; others may require adjustments in resource allocations. In all cases, suggestions should be viewed as possible alternatives, with individual institutions creating their own distinct formulas for deliberate and sustained initiatives to integrate part-time faculty into the institutional fabric. Proposed action plans in this volume have three key characteristics in common. They are all

- Positive in attempting to improve conditions, relations, performance, and quality
- Pragmatic in using commonsense and easy-to-apply practices
- Proactive in offering thoughtful and creative approaches

The potential and real value of any action plan depends on local conditions and is subject to local interpretation. While one would hope that many of the suggestions contained in this volume will be adopted, specific combinations, timelines, and adaptations will vary and will, one hopes, be the result of institutional dialogue, collaborative efforts, and an honest attempt to improve. Financial and political considerations have their place once any policy, process, or practice has been determined to have merit in furthering the basic goals of the institution. To start the conversation by enumerating all the factors preventing a plan from being implemented is insincere and self-defeating. Success in any culture shift includes, first, the ability to articulate a positive vision; second, assessment of available resources and possible challenges to its realization; and third, a well-considered and -articulated plan to address and overcome challenges.

The theme of *Connections* has been chosen to underscore the importance of integrating all who teach at an institution into a vibrant and viable community. While some connections clearly belong in one arena or another, many belong in more than one. Such overlapping is impossible to avoid and, in fact, may underscore the importance of collaboration. A 2000 survey of 1,500 full- and part-time faculty nationwide, found that

> Although part-time faculty are generally well-qualified to perform their duties . . . it can be argued that part-timers are more weakly linked to their students, colleagues and . . . institutions than full-timers . . . less familiar with the availability of campus services [and so] . . . less likely to sustain extracurricular student-faculty interactions.[1]

Adjunct = Appendage, Not of the core

Something joined or added to another thing but
not essentially a part of it

(Merriam-Webster's Collegiate Dictionary,
10th Edition, 1998.)

Part-time college faculty, variously referred to as *adjunct, part-timers,* or *contingent faculty,* now comprise almost half of all instructional professionals at American colleges and universities. U.S. Department of Education data reveal that in 1970, 22 percent of faculty were considered part time, and in 1987, the proportion rose to 38 percent.[2] In 1998, it rose to 43 percent.[3] The numbers are not necessarily evenly distributed across disciplines and may be more significant in some disciplines and fields. For example, according to a statement issued in 1999 by the Coalition on the Academic Workforce, made up of 25 academic societies,[4] part-time faculty and graduate students accounted for approximately 85.4 percent of all instructors in independent English composition courses, while in department-based English composition courses they accounted for 63.7 percent of all instructors (graduate students accounted for 15–20 percent in both cases). The steady increase in the number of part-time faculty and their proportion among faculty is rooted in several developments, yet the outcomes are the same—an ever-growing distinction between two segments of faculty, the full-timers and the part-timers.

All types of higher education institutions employ large numbers of part-time faculty—research universities, four-year colleges, community and junior colleges, and vocational and trade colleges. While proportions may vary among types of institutions, the general trend and reasons for the proliferation of the use of part-time faculty are quite similar.

Factors Contributing to the Increase in Adjunct Faculty Use

It does not appear that the adjunct faculty phenomenon evolved by design. Rather, as in so many other industries, what was for a long time a small, insignificant number of part-time workers has now developed to a significant size, presenting in the process new challenges and opportunities. Some of the reasons for the proliferation of part-time faculty include the following:

- *Budgetary constraints and expediencies.* In many settings, part-time faculty are perceived to be "cheap labor" in that they are paid for teaching by the course, usually at a rate significantly lower than that of a full-time instructor. It is a simple line item, one that is not usually accompanied by expenditures for benefits. Additionally, the overhead cost of employing part-time faculty is obviously lower than that of full-time faculty since, typically, few or no support services are provided. As budgets shrink or programs expand without corresponding budgetary increases, hiring part-time faculty is seen both as a prudent investment and an easy solution.

- *Increased enrollments.* Enrollment patterns reflect social realities—birthrates; economic gyrations downward and upward; popularity of specific disciplines, professions, or industries; internal migrations, increased immigration, etc. Enrollment levels may shift dramatically within a short period, so addressing them through the use of part-time faculty becomes an expedient and attractive option.

- *Course enrollment fluctuations.* Especially in core and remedial courses, enrollments tend to be uneven at different times of the year. Most students still tend to enter college in the fall, so fall schedules typically include many more sections of a course than do spring schedules. At large institutions that accept a sizable freshman student cohort during the summer, that time of year presents its own challenges as full-time faculty may not be available due to vacation schedules or because they are typically on a nine-month contract. Part-time faculty are available on short notice to teach unplanned, extra sections and can be given short notice, without political fallout, when sections are cancelled due to low enrollment.

- *A changing student population.* With a marked increase in the number of nontraditional college students—adults completing unfinished degrees, second career pursuers, retirees, and upwardly mobile professionals—demand for expanded evening and weekend schedules has followed. While full-time faculty's availability to address the increased number of courses and course sections may be limited by collective bargaining agreements or contracts, part-time faculty welcome the opportunity to increase their teaching load.

- *Diverse definitions of the academic enterprise.* Different types of institutions see their primary mission and the roles of faculty in diverse ways. While universities and some four-year colleges define faculty roles as a triad of teaching, scholarship, and service, community colleges and many liberal arts colleges see teaching as the primary, if not always the only, role of faculty. It is not surprising, therefore, that the number of part-time faculty teaching at community colleges tended to be relatively large long before it became obvious at other types of institution.

- *Desire to expand course offerings.* As enrollments have grown and students' expectations have changed, institutions have been expanding the variety of disciplines they offer and increasing the diversity of available majors far beyond the traditional arts and sciences core. This proliferation of disciplines has required recruitment of experts as faculty, especially in the professional fields, spanning the full gamut from business, health, and education to hospitality management and public policy. As institutions have become more comfortable with the use of part-time faculty who are full-time professionals elsewhere, other, more "traditional" disciplines have also been supplementing their full-time pool with part-time faculty.

- *Remediation and basic skills courses.* With increased enrollments and the expectation that a college degree is the passport to lifelong success comes an influx of students who may require remedial or basic courses to enhance skills formerly addressed in high school. Many of these courses, especially in math and English, are either part of the core curriculum or are prerequisites to core courses, so their enrollments have swelled to the point where full-time faculty members are not able to cover the need. Enter the part-time faculty, who are well qualified to teach at this level, and who, like their colleagues in the professional disciplines, may be full-time successful professionals such as journalists or government researchers.

- *Programmatic flexibility.* Changes in the national economy bring with them changes in the skills and knowledge expected from college graduates. These fluctuations are becoming more frequent, as the recent situation in the high-tech field clearly illustrates. Where in the past such fluctuations may have occurred over a relatively long period, their increased frequency seen in recent times means that institutions need to be able to respond rapidly. The use of part-time faculty allows for more short-term planning and for quick response to unplanned demand.

- *Flexibility of place.* Part-time faculty can be hired to teach at off-campus sites, including business or public facilities such as libraries, or remote locations too far for commuting. While such arrangements are highly desirable to the nontraditional pool of students, full-time faculty do not necessarily favor them.
- *A recruitment pool for full-time positions.* In some but not too many instances, mostly in community college and liberal arts college settings, part-time faculty are hired and perceived as potential full-time faculty. By meeting institutional expectations and establishing collegial relationships with supervisors and full-time faculty, they may have the edge when full-time positions become available. Their attraction to the institution is not only in their familiarity with it, but also in potentially lower recruitment costs.
- *Clinical supervision.* Many professionally oriented disciplines require their students to complete an internship or field experience. These practical learning experiences are usually co-supervised by teaching faculty and practicing professionals. While not always classified as part-time faculty, practicing professionals are called on to perform pedagogical duties such as one-on-one instruction, group discussions, mentoring, assignment evaluation, testing, and grading.
- *Get around tenure.* In some instances, a case could be made that an increase in the number of part-time faculty is a reflection of institutional desire to reduce the number of tenured faculty. It reflects both political and economic reasoning and, due to its controversial nature, is not often discussed openly.
- *Enhance affirmative action profile.* As the proportion of female and minority part-time faculty is relatively high, hiring them may provide good "formal data" when combined with the full-time faculty pool. Figures collected by the U.S. Department of Education show, for instance, that in 1991, full-time faculty ranks included 169,410 women and 366,213 men, while part-time faculty ranks included 131,243 women and 159,386 men. Similarly, in 1995, full-time faculty ranks included 190,672 women and 360,150 men, compared to 178,141 women and 202,743 men in part-time faculty ranks.[5]

Who Are the Part-time Faculty?

Part-time faculty fall into three broad categories:

1. Professionals active in their fields, with full-time careers, who teach a course or two "on the side." Their motivations may include interest in keeping up with the academic side of the profession, altruism—helping to prepare the next generation of professionals, or recruitment by schools that want to provide their students with early exposure to practitioners in the disciplines. They can also serve as "goodwill ambassadors" for the school in the larger community, advocating for the school at their place of work, civic organizations, local government, etc.

2. Academicians who for one reason or another have put together the equivalent of a full-time career out of teaching part time at several schools. Referred to sometimes as *roads scholars* or *freeway scholars*, these part-time faculty often have the same educational credentials as full-time faculty do. Some of these individuals are happy with their lifestyle; many are not.

3. Individuals who are not interested in a full-time career, and who teach for the joy of teaching or to stay involved with the discipline. This group may include retired professionals or academicians, full-time mothers, or graduate students.

Individuals are motivated to become part-time faculty for a variety of reasons. Among them,

> reasons for teaching are as diverse as the students they serve. Some see adjunct teaching as a possible entry to a full-time faculty position. Some are merely trying to bring in a little extra money. Some—attorneys, business people, police officers—are teaching as a service and a way to give back to the community that supports them. Others, such as nurses and allied health professionals, have a much needed skill to share. Secondary teachers may like the challenge and change of working with adults. Still others teach because they like being on a college campus.[6]

Common to all three groups is the lack of some basic working conditions taken for granted by their full-time counterparts. Part-time faculty often

- Receive no health, disability, or retirement benefits
- Are not provided with basic support items such as office space, computer access, library privileges, parking privileges, access to audiovisual equipment, and duplicating services
- Cannot count on secretarial assistance
- Are not part of program, curriculum, and course development processes
- Do not have ready access to faculty and professional development opportunities

Why Are the Part-time Faculty Challenges So Important?

Part-time faculty have been concerned primarily with pay equity and benefits; however, much has also been articulated about their working conditions, their relationship to and with the institutions they serve, and the part-time faculty's place within the academic community.

Professional and labor organizations have taken note of this trend and have begun to explore, and sometimes demand, a change in practices related to part-time faculty. Slowly but steadily part-time faculty are gaining the right to unionize, in private as well as in public institutions.[7] Most recently, courts have ruled that part-time faculty cannot be classified as temporary workers.[8] Accrediting bodies, regional as well as professional, while establishing guidelines for the proportion of faculty that can be part-time, and while requiring that certain performance criteria such as office hours, be met, have not been too concerned with part-time faculty's working conditions, especially not with their pay levels, benefits, or support systems. The American Association of University Professors (AAUP) has articulated similar recommendations for limiting the number of part-time faculty:

> We recommend as guidelines that institutions limit the use of special appointments and part-time non-tenure track faculty to no more than 15 percent of the total instruction within the institution, and no more than 25 percent of the total instruction within any given department.[9]

The most compelling reason for placing high priority on part-time faculty issues should not, however, be an external or even an internal threat to unionize or litigate. Rather, the motivation for creating, developing, and maintaining an inclusive teaching community should be the realization that part-time faculty, in smaller or larger proportions, are here to stay and in many cases serve as the lifeline of many schools. Therefore, they should be integrated into the institutional fiber in a manner that will provide opportunities for improved academic performance on all fronts. As Vince Tinto eloquently states,

> In a very real sense the faculty and staff serve as both representatives and mediators of the social and intellectual life of the institution. Their actions are important indicators to students of both the quality of that life and the degree to which the institution is concerned with the life of students.[10]

Three recent developments underscore the importance of the issues presented here. Each of them took place in a unique setting:

- The U.S. Department of Education released data showing that part-time positions form the fastest-growing segment of the academic job market.[11]
- At the biennial conference of the Coalition of Contingent Academic Labor in Vancouver, B.C., in August 2006, AAUP president Cary Nelson, representing the United States, said he hoped that American adjuncts will assert themselves in their local unions so their important voice will be heard.[12]
- The AAUP announced in September 2006 that it would be asking members to approve a detailed set of guidelines for adjunct instructors. Its three main provisions are:
  - All part-time faculty members should receive the terms of appointment in writing and should have a right to a hearing in case of dismissal before the end of the period of appointment.
  - Those who have served for three or more terms within three years should receive written notice of reappointment or non-reappointment no later than one month before the end of the existing term of appointment; receive written reasons, if requested, in case of non-reappointment; and have a right to appeal a non-reappointment that appears to be discriminatory, based significantly on considerations violating academic freedom, or attributable to inadequate consideration.
  - Prior to consideration of reappointment beyond a seventh year, part-time faculty members who have taught at least twelve courses

or six terms within those seven years shall be provided a comprehensive review with a view toward (1) appointment with part-time
tenure where such exists, (2) appointment with part-time continuing service, or (3) non-reappointment.[13]

This is a dynamic environment in which the many interested parties seem to
be asserting themselves in new and ever more forceful ways.

Notes

1. Schuet, P. (2002). Instructional Practices of Part-Time and Full-Time Faculty. In C. L. Outcalt (ed.), *New Directions for Community Colleges: N. 118. Community College Faculty: Characteristics, Practices, and Challenges*. San Francisco, CA:
Jossey-Bass, p. 44.

2. Wilson, Robin. (1996, June 14). Scholars Off the Tenure Track Wonder If
They'll Ever Get On. *The Chronicle of Higher Education*, June 14, 1996 (http://
chronicle.com/che-data/articles.dir/art-42.dir/issue40dir/40a01201.htm).

3. U.S. Department of Education, National Center for Education Statistics.
(2001, April). *Background Characteristics, Work Activities, and Compensation of Faculty and Instructional Staff in Postsecondary Institutions: Fall 1998* (NCES 2001-152).

4. American Historical Association. (1999, fall). *Who Is Teaching in U.S. College
Classrooms? A Collaborative Study of Undergraduate Faculty*. Washington, DC: Author (http://www.theaha.org/caw/pressrelease.htm).

5. Schneider, Alison. (1998, March). More Professors Are Working Part Time,
and More Teach at 2-year Colleges. *The Chronicle of Higher Education*, A15.

6. Wallin, D. L. [**Au: insert date of publication**]. Valuing Professional Colleagues: Adjunct Faculty in Community and Technical Colleges. *Community College
Journal of Research and Practice, 28*, 2.

7. Smallwood, Scott. (2002, April 22). Adjuncts at New York U. Have 3 Choices
in Union Vote. *The Chronicle of Higher Education Daily News* (http://chronicle.com/
daily/2002/04/2002042203n.htm).

8. Fogg, Piper. (2002, April 22). Court Upholds Ruling That Allows Adjuncts
at Keene State College to Unionize. *The Chronicle of Higher Education* (http://
chronicle.com/daily/2002/04/2002042202n.htm).

9. American Association of University Professors (AAUP). (1993, June). *The
Status of Non-Tenure-Track Faculty, A Report of the Association's Committee on Part-
Time and Non-Tenure-Track Appointments*, p. 44 (also available at http://www.aaup
.org/statements/Redbook/Rbnonten.htm).

10. Tinto, Vincent. (1987). *Leaving College: Rethinking the Causes and Cures of
Student Attrition*. Chicago: University of Chicago Press.

11. National Center for Education Statistics. (2006). *Changes in Staff Distribution*

and Salaries of Full-Time Employees in Postsecondary Institutions: Fall 1993–2003.
Washington, DC: Author.

12. Gravois, John. (2006, August). Adjunct Professors Discuss Labor Issues and College "Corporatization" at Biennial Conference. *The Chronicle of Higher Education,* A15.

13. American Association of University Professors. (2006, September) AAUP Proposes New Institutional Regulation on Part-Time Appointments (http://www.aaup .org/AAUP/newsroom/pressreleases/PRContingentRIR.htm).

TO THE INSTITUTION

Steps in Creating an Inclusive Teaching Community

Action Plans

The Challenge

The number of part-time faculty may be leveling off, but their presence is permanent. To provide, support, or sustain quality educational programs, all faculty members need to be part of their institution's creative, intellectual, and administrative fabric. To meet the challenge, an institution should create and foster an organizational climate and culture that are:

- *Inclusive.* The roles of all faculty who are engaged in teaching are identical. What may distinguish between and among them is the proportionate time commitment. Similarly, aside from unique scholarly activity requirements (such as for tenure and promotion), nonteaching roles of teachers, such as participation in institutional life, student advising, and professional contributions, are expected from and valued by all.
- *Supportive.* The necessary working conditions and tools are provided equitably so that every teacher can do an outstanding job. Acknowledgment of contributions and quality is provided readily as are opportunities for professional growth.
- *Collegial.* The institution promotes interaction among part-time faculty members and between full-time and part-time faculty. Support and professional staff members provide the necessary services to all faculty without distinction.

Many and varied initiatives can and must be undertaken to achieve long-range integration of part-time faculty. Institutional commitment to change in philosophy and practice will spawn numerous initiatives that are

1. Collaborative in nature, involving many and diverse stakeholders so that rather than mandating change by fiat, true partnerships are evolved to assure both acceptance and longevity

2. Ongoing and evolving, allowing for the gradual introduction of new concepts and practices, continuous assessment of effectiveness, and periodic adjustments, if needed

3. Open and informative, keeping all constituencies aware of needs, approaches, and results

4. Quality driven, paying vigilant attention to the stated goals and the appropriateness of the tools selected to achieve these goals

The integration of part-time faculty into the total institutional fabric is a major undertaking and one for which few models are available. Each institution, because of its own unique character, mission, and practices, will approach the challenge in a unique way. As is the case with all successful strategic planning, the process will involve not just the resolve to "do something," but a thoughtful and deliberate set of steps that will increase the likelihood of success. While the inspiration and the call to action should come from the highest levels of administration so that they are both credible and supported with the appropriate tools and resources, the critical work needs to be done by members of all segments and at all levels within the institution. Some initiatives may have to be experimental in nature while others may be launched as permanent features. Experimental approaches may be able to acquire funding through grant programs such as the Fund for the Improvement of Postsecondary Education (FIPSE), while more permanent programs may be of interest to donors who would like to have their name associated with a novel and much appreciated project. It would be natural and tempting to start with those initiatives that may require the fewest new or redirected resources; however, for any program to be successful in the long run, the "big picture" must be established first, with corresponding short- and long-range plans articulated as well. Sandra E. Elman, executive director of the Northwest Commission on Colleges and Universities, states,

> In short, colleges and universities must either work to create an institutional culture that embraces part-time faculty as credible, legitimate members of the academic profession or else not hire them at all. Failure to create an institutional culture that enables part-time faculty to be effective not only compromises the educational experience of students, it is not equitable. Absent such a culture, any use of part-time faculty risks undermining the integrity of the institution.[1]

The following Action Plans are presented as starting points for institutional discussion and consideration. While there is some logic behind the sequencing, it is not meant to be prescriptive. Rather, the list should provide some assistance in organizing and prioritizing the process of change. In some instances, more than one possible approach is described. Ultimately, though, the programs that will evolve will likely display their own character and flavor.

Action Plans

What's in a Name?

Classification of Part-time Faculty within the Institution

Faculty members who are not on the tenure track and who teach less than a full load of courses are referred to in several ways—*part-time faculty*, *adjunct faculty*, and *contingency faculty* are the most common names. While there is no clear agreement on what these names represent, in some cases the distinctions can be significant. For instance, in some institutions *part-time* refers to faculty who occupy a *faculty line* on a part-time basis and who may, therefore, receive proportionate benefits, while *adjunct* refers to individuals who are paid out of general operating funds and do not receive any benefits.

Whatever the terminology, it is important to agree on a single name, one that conveys inclusion and participation rather than exclusion and lower status. Suggested titles include *associated faculty* and *affiliated faculty* when the context is one in which full-time faculty are clearly distinguished as separate. Such may be the case in environments in which labor unions include only full-time faculty. The following formats strive for a higher level of inclusiveness:

1. *Classification by rank.* All faculty are categorized by a single set of titles—instructor, lecturer, assistant professor, associate professor, full professor—that reflect achievements and quality of performance rather than proportion of employment. While the requirements for each level may vary from tenure track to non-tenure-track faculty, a set of expectations, standards, policies, and evaluative criteria are in place and are applied uniformly across discipline lines.

2. *Classification by seniority.* All faculty are categorized by the longevity of their employment at the institution (although credit for earlier work elsewhere may be considered) and quality of performance. The Vancouver, British Columbia Community College, for instance, classifies all faculty as *term faculty* when they are first employed. They are hired on a probationary basis, subject to ongoing summative evaluation, and are reviewed for permanent status after a prescribed number of years. At the same institution, *permanent faculty* are those who have performed successfully as term faculty; their continued employment is contractual.[2]

3. *Separate but parallel classification.* In this format, full-time faculty are classified in the traditional mode, that is, *instructor, assistant professor, associate professor,* and *full professor.* Non full-time faculty may be classified independently, but on a parallel scale, such as *assistant lecturer, associate lecturer, senior lecturer,* and so on. There is room for some creativity in defining such titles. The reason for distinct scales is that the requirements for promotion are likely to be different for full-time and part-time faculty.

Note: For the sake of consistency, the term *part-time faculty* is used throughout this book.

Coordination

A sense of belonging and loyalty by part-time faculty can and should be fostered on two levels—departmental (discussed in Connection 2) and institutional. As so many part-time faculty teach at either uncommon hours or days or at off-campus locations, the challenge of inclusiveness cannot be underestimated. Although their first contact with the institution may be through a specific academic department or program, their success ultimately depends on their relationship with the institution as a whole. The two coordinating approaches listed below, a coordinating board and a part-time faculty affairs coordinator, can be done separately or in tandem with one another. If only one of the two approaches is implemented, however, the functions listed for both should be joined into a single agenda.

Part-time Faculty Coordinating Board

A group of key individuals representing all segments of the institution—part-time faculty, full-time faculty, and administrators—is convened to address, on an ongoing basis, issues related to employment of part-time faculty. In the existence of a Faculty Senate and/or Faculty Union, these bodies must be represented on this board. The following are some of the key functions of the Coordinating Board:

- Develop an institutional vision and a mission statement for the employment of part-time faculty that is consistent with institutional goals to provide high-quality education and supportive of an integrated, professional faculty.
- Develop and regularly review policies and procedures for the management of part-time faculty.
- Serve in an advisory capacity to the administration, academic units, and other campus organizations on matters involving part-time faculty.
- Hear grievances and recommend resolutions for issues unique to part-time faculty (in the absence of union representation), such as priority assignments, promotions, academic freedom, and compensation levels.
- Advocate for part-time faculty in arenas such as the Faculty Senate, the Faculty Union, administrative committees, and college/unit committees.
- Develop and make recommendations about work environment issues, including the following (see a more detailed discussion later in this chapter):
  - Access to communication systems
    - *Phones.* Part-time faculty can conduct teaching-related business with students and colleagues via an institutional phone (rather than their private or cell phone).
    - *E-mail.* An address within the institutional system is provided so that part-time faculty can conduct institutional business in a secure and reliable environment and have access to important institutional information as well as information directed specifically to them.
  - Year-round library privileges with access to on-site and online resources to be used for preparation and for teaching
  - Highly reduced or prorated parking fees

- Membership in the Faculty Club and similar voluntary organizations
- Discounts at the campus bookstore
- Discounts for campus activities and services at the same level granted to full-time faculty and staff
- Educate the campus community and assist in developing mechanisms for the inclusion of part-time faculty representatives on campuswide, unit, and departmental committees.

Part-time Faculty Affairs Coordinator

Preferably based in the academic affairs division, this professional serves as the central address for the day-to-day management of part-time faculty matters. The individual serving in this capacity should

- Have experience in teaching as a part-time faculty member
- Report directly to the chief academic officer of the institution (provost, VP, academic affairs, etc.)
- Have the trust and support of part-time faculty, department chairpersons, deans, and other decision makers who are involved with part-time faculty issues
- Serve on but not chair the Part-time Faculty Coordinating Board

The Coordinator's functions are numerous and diverse. Some functions can be identified and specified upfront; others may evolve over time and with experience. These functions would see the Coordinator:

- Propose policies and procedures
- Serve as ombudsman
- Coordinate implementation of policies and procedures
- Negotiate with campus organizations, such as the technology group, for access and services by part-time faculty
- Advise the Coordinating Board on needed policies as well as policy and procedure modifications
- Coordinate needs determination, recruitment, and selection of part-time faculty
- Maintain data such as part-time faculty lists and contact information

Needs Determination, Recruitment, and Selection

Part of the reason for discrepancies among part-time faculty hiring practices, salaries, working conditions, and, consequently, quality control issues within institutions is the decentralized nature of the processes. So often, each department, and sometimes each program within a given department, recruits, hires, negotiates, and contracts with its own part-time faculty. While frontline departmental and program involvement with part-time faculty is essential for a successful practice, as is discussed later in this volume, the institution as a whole needs to provide leadership in these areas.

Needs Determination

Instructional needs, short- and long-term, should be determined on an ongoing, annual basis. Just as central administration allocates full-time faculty positions based on departmental projections, demographic considerations, space availability, and changing demands, so, too, should part-time faculty needs be part of the institutional planning process. Each department has the best information about its own staffing patterns—how many and what courses it wishes to offer, teaching assignments of permanent full-time faculty, accounting for sabbatical and other leaves, or teaching assignments of graduate teaching assistants where they are available. However, the burden of maintaining full-time to part-time faculty ratios, for instance, is an institutional requirement, dictated by accreditation requirements, boards, and other stakeholders. The academic affairs division is usually charged with this task, and a planning office, if one exists, often handles it.

One of the reasons for the proliferation of part-time faculty is that they are a convenience, especially as last-minute appointments. Such appointments can be capricious and not necessarily in the best interests of the institution; they can also lead to situations in which more than half of the instructional staff in a program is comprised of part-time faculty—not necessarily the best or most desired situation. Just as departments need to submit their classroom space requirements regularly, expected needs for part-time faculty should also be reported at the planning stage.

A solid planning process includes

- Determination of the desired institutional ratio of part-time to full-time faculty

- Determination of the relative departmental ratios of part-time and full-time faculty, taking into consideration "service course" demands such as English composition and introductory math
- Determination of basic qualifications and standards for part-time teaching positions
- Establishment of hiring process guidelines

Recruitment

Creation of a stable and sufficient pool of potential part-time faculty is another step toward quality teaching. Rather than scrambling at the last minute to hire anyone who is willing to take on the responsibility, departments need to maintain lists not only of those part-time faculty who have already taught for them, but of potential teachers as well. The best time to start developing such a list is not when a shortage occurs but when selection can be done in a reasonable, equitable, and systematic manner.

A pool of candidates for part-time faculty positions can be established and maintained in several ways:

- *Job fairs held at the institution.* This is a great way to bring the community to the campus, highlight academic programs, and connect the school to the community in a tangible way.
- *Recruitment within local industries and businesses.* The Chamber of Commerce is a good starting point, and ongoing partnerships through individual human resources departments are also productive. Businesses value employees who teach at colleges and universities as such experience validates the companies' professional standing, so they are another useful recruitment venue.
- *Recruitment at area high schools.* Many high school teachers are well qualified to teach college courses, especially at the lower division and in service courses. An organized effort in this area can also create opportunities for dialogue between high school and college instructors—something sorely missed in many instances.
- *Cooperative recruitment with neighboring institutions.* Staffing needs may vary from school to school, and where one institution may need extra English instructors this year, another may not and may be able to share resources.
- *Recruitment within government agencies and nonprofit organizations.*

Both of these employ many highly qualified individuals who for one reason or another have chosen a career other than full-time college teaching. Yet some may be interested in a part-time faculty position.

- *Advertisements through local and regional media.* Disseminating a list of the various departments and programs that hire part-time faculty is a great way to publicize the many areas the institution covers. Small, classified ads rarely get sufficient attention.

Selection

Just as departments and programs determine who will ultimately teach as full-time faculty, they also need to have the final say in who will teach part time. However, it is the institution's responsibility to establish and enforce some basic standards. While many of these standards are dictated by accrediting organizations, they tend to reflect minimal requirements; the institution is free to raise the bar. The American Association of University Professors (AAUP) recommends a set of "guidelines for good practices":

- Selection and hiring based on clear criteria with standards consistent with institutional mission
- Active recruitment and selection of the best available candidates to minimize fragmented assignments
- Assurance that qualified part-time faculty will be considered fairly for tenure-track opportunities
- Long-term planning whenever possible to provide extended terms of appointment consistent with institutional needs to support continued involvement with students and colleagues[3]

Standards and requirements ought to be established and communicated clearly repeatedly throughout the institution. Part-time faculty hiring and employment patterns differ from those of full-time faculty in that the latter are usually based on collective bargaining agreements, state mandates, and other standards, while hiring part-time faculty is left to the discretion of individual departments. Establishment of part-time faculty selection standards should be a collaborative process among academic units to ensure that specialized needs and diverse disciplines are considered and accounted for. Some of the criteria established as part of the selection process may include:

- Previous teaching experience at this institution and elsewhere
- Education and degrees obtained
- Scholarly activities
- Professional experience with bearing on the teaching assignment
- Maximum credit hours permissible per term or year
- Concurrent teaching assignments at other institutions
- "Priority" assignments for long-term, high-quality instructors

Once basic requirements have been met, selection of new part-time faculty to actually teach should adhere to certain basic procedural standards:

- A personal interview with a direct supervisor
- A short, 15-minute presentation (micro-teaching) in front of several full-time and part-time colleagues
- Where appropriate, a spontaneous writing sample

Contracts

As is the case with most contractual relationships, part-time faculty teaching contracts need to be issued and signed in a timely manner; they are the most tangible connector between the institution and its part-time faculty. A typical part-time teaching contract is issued for the semester involved. To help in creating an inclusive environment, such contracts need to

1. Be issued before the start of a teaching assignment, preferably at least several weeks ahead, so that proper course preparation can take place
2. Be issued for the entire academic year for those part-time faculty with a successful record at the institution

When constructed properly, both single-term and full-year contracts can contain language that allows for voiding the contract in case a course does not have the required minimum enrollment.

For longtime, qualified part-time faculty with a record of successful teaching, a multiyear contract is a viable option. Such contracts can be issued for any term, possibly two to five years. Long-term contracts for high-quality faculty ensure both continuity and quality.

The content of contracts is usually prescribed by either the state or the institution's governing body. In many cases, however, the language of the contract is rather generic and does not include items that are especially important if part-time faculty are to become integrated into the institution. Contracts need to be as inclusive as possible, covering key parameters while not getting bogged down in minutiae. Contracts should include:

- Clear expectations and assignments, including in-class teaching, availability for student contact, and course preparation
- Fair labor protection information
- Expectations for participation beyond the classroom—committees, departmental meetings, student advising, faculty development activities
- Reference to the Faculty Handbook, including acknowledgment that it has been read and clearly understood

A fair, reasonable, and timely contract can go a long way toward fostering connectivity between the institution and its part-time faculty, especially long-term ones, increased accessibility to students, and fostering an environment of quality teaching.

Financial Matters

Much has been said and written about the financial realities of part-time faculty employment. Still operating under the assumption that the part-time faculty phenomenon is a temporary one, many institutions have shied away from developing coherent institutional fiscal structures that provide consistency, fairness, and continuity. The prevailing model for paying part-time faculty is based on a per course fee, with a wide range of approximately $1,200–$3,500 per three-credit course, with some very specialized courses paying more. While the range itself could be a subject for debate, what makes the issue even more compelling is the disparity of pay among departments within the same institution; while some departments maintain firm pay scales, others are open to individual negotiation. Two distinct areas of financial matters need to be addressed: pay structures and pay increment structures.

The first concern should be to develop and implement a uniform pay scale and pay system across the institution. Granted, it will take a fair amount of internal negotiation, but if nothing else, it eliminates situations in which one department competes against another for the services of the same instructor, and the "winner" is the department that pays more. There are two key options for establishing consistent pay scales:

Pay per Course

A basic course is defined as a three-credit, three-contact-hours per week course. At present, most per course fees barely cover the time spent in direct contact with students. When determining pay per course, the following elements should also be accounted for:

- Preparation time and review and evaluation of student work, usually calculated as three hours for each contact hour
- Office hours—they are often mandated by accrediting and state agencies but are seldom required, much less compensated
- Student advising—when it is an expectation, part-time faculty should be compensated for it (there is a broader discussion elsewhere in this book of the possible role part-time faculty can play in student advisement)
- Payment for preparation time when a course is cancelled at the last minute

Proportionate Pay

Using full-time faculty's pay scale as a guide—accounting only for those portions of the job that part-time faculty actually perform—part-time faculty's pay is calculated as a straight percentage of the whole. While reasonable in theory, this option can be complex when part-time faculty are expected to do more than just show up for class. It may require the development of several "tracks" to account for diverse combinations of duties.

The second area of financial consideration is that of pay increments. As part-time faculty establish a successful record, their pay should be adjusted upward. Here, too, one of two approaches can be selected, or the two can be combined.

1. *Cost of Living Adjustments.* Using the same adjustment levels and frequency as those for full-time faculty, part-time faculty's salaries can be adjusted periodically.

2. *A Step System.* Based on successful performance, preset steps are followed in determining pay scales. In this arrangement, two key factors
need to be considered—the starting "step," a baseline for all starting
part-time faculty with similar qualifications, and predetermined periodic increases. The following is a hypothetical illustration of a step
system:

Step 1	$xxx per credit hour	MA, new hire, little or no experience
Step 2	$xxx + $50 per credit hour	
Step 3	$xxx + $100 per credit hour	MSWs automatically start here
Step 4	$xxx + $150 per credit hour	PhDs, MFAs automatically start here
Step 5	$xxx + $200 per credit hour	
Step 6	$xxx + $250 per credit hour	

Part-time faculty automatically move up one step after teaching six semesters with a minimum of six credit hours per semester. Part-time faculty
teaching fewer than six credit hours per semester are bumped up to the next
step when they reach 36 cumulative hours. A step up takes place for the fall
semester only, no bumps occur for the spring semester. Those part-time faculty with at least three years of teaching experience at the college level, and
in the same discipline, can start at one step higher than novices. Market conditions will dictate the starting step as well as periodic adjustments of the
entire scale. Such adjustments may be tied to and be a percentage of full-
time faculty's base salaries.

Whichever approach is implemented, consistency and predictability are
key factors in ensuring equitability of pay among part-time faculty and
among departments.

Benefits

Three distinct approaches, and combinations thereof, can be used to provide
part-time faculty with health and related benefits (other benefits will be discussed elsewhere in this book). These are discussed below.

Proportionate Benefits

This approach provides part-time faculty with a percentage of full-time faculty's benefits identical to the proportional size of their position. For example, if a part-time instructor's load is considered to be one-third that of a full-time instructor, the part-timer receives one-third of the benefits provided to a full-timer. Stipulations can be made as to the length of employment required to become eligible for benefits. As is the case with full-time faculty, part-time faculty would contribute toward the cost of benefits, possibly at a higher level. Proportionate benefits can also be structured so that basic health insurance is provided, but with no supplemental options.

No-cost or Low-cost Benefits

Some benefits involve no or minimal out-of-pocket expense for the institution and are made available to part-time faculty on the same basis as they are to full-time faculty. The following is a list of such benefits.

- Access to a credit union
- Access to financial advice
- Sick leave at the rate of one day per three credit course
- Tax-deferred annuity option by which a part-time instructor may elect to have a permissible portion of pay withheld prior to taxes. This option can be of great benefit to part-time faculty in that it reduces taxable income, and earnings are tax-deferred.
- Access to retirement programs such as those offered by TIAA-CREF and other companies, to be paid solely by the part-time instructor
- Purchase of savings bonds with pretax money. The income earned on such bonds is exempt from local and state taxes, and federal taxes may be deferred until the bonds are redeemed or no longer earn interest. An additional benefit of this program is that interest on savings bonds used to pay for education may be tax exempt.
- Coverage by worker's compensation in the same manner as hourly workers, graduate assistants, and postdoctoral fellows
- Access to campus health and wellness facilities and programs

Group Benefits

Using the buying power and clout of large groups, the institution, on behalf of its part-time faculty (and possibly other noncovered groups such as graduate assistants), can negotiate favorable programs with health insurance companies, retirement/annuity companies such as TIAA-CREF, and other providers. Policies are paid solely by part-time faculty, who are likely to save considerable amounts by buying into a group policy.

Orientation to the Institution

For many part-time faculty, walking into the classroom for the first session is only the second time they set foot on campus or in a satellite facility; the first time was when they were hired, if that was done on school grounds. Surely, that is not the best way to make meaningful connections between part-time faculty and the institution, or between part-time faculty and the students. Students perceive their instructors, part time or otherwise, to represent the school when it comes to knowledge of policies and procedures, performance standards, access to student services, and a general understanding of institutional culture. Part-time faculty who have not been oriented to the institution can hardly be expected to provide students with valuable support in these areas.

Many schools now have well-established orientation programs for new (full-time) faculty and for support staff; they may vary in length, scope, and intensity, but they all have the common goal of helping new employees become familiar with the culture, values, resources, and requirements of the organization. A similar approach to new part-time faculty can go a long way toward integrating them into the community and institutional life and, consequently, promoting collegiality and quality. Part-time faculty who hold full-time jobs elsewhere or develop the equivalent of a full-time teaching career by teaching part time in several schools are motivated not only by financial considerations and by the gratification of knowing that they are engaged in an important undertaking; a sense of affiliation and the resulting ability to represent the institution well are also important. That sense of affiliation should start before the first class session.

The sections below describe the essentials of a part-time faculty orientation program. No time frameworks are given as that is a variable affected by the number of part-time faculty involved, the size of the institution, and scheduling considerations.

Orientation Program Outline

Involvement

The top academic administrator, such as the provost, should convene the orientation through individual invitation letters and should open the procedures. Part-time faculty need to know that they and their contributions are valued at the highest levels of administration. Deans' and department chairpersons' participation, at least by way of introductions, is important for the same reason. To save time and energy, chairpersons can introduce the part-time faculty teaching in their departments, including their credentials such as academic degrees, scholarly achievements, and professional experience if their main employment is in nonacademic settings. The prevailing invisibility of part-time faculty leads many to assume that part-time faculty possess minimal qualifications when, in reality, many of them could probably compete successfully with full-time faculty.

Campus professionals providing faculty and student support services should also participate. Their involvement can be of two types:

- A resource organization fair—information tables displaying the services provided, reference handouts, and representatives who can answer questions. This is an efficient way to acquaint participants with many services in a short time.
- Presentation of information during the formal segments of the program. While this approach may be very suitable for some topics (see below), it may create a nonparticipatory type of program.

Key Content Areas

- Institutional structure. This is especially beneficial for those whose primary professional lives are not in an academic environment.
- Basic teaching and learning process. This segment would include discussion of such important areas as
  - Learning styles
  - Syllabus development
  - Establishment of course requirements, if not standard, and the rationale for requirements, if standardized
  - Guidance in resources selection—textbooks, Web materials, etc.
  - Assignment development
  - Testing and assessment strategies

- ■ Evaluation and grading policies and standards
- ■ Promotion of academic honesty
- Administrative procedures
- Diversity issues
- Sexual harassment policies—a separate training session may be mandated, but general parameters should be discussed

Format

An interactive, participant-centered structure is essential (as it is in teaching) for part-time faculty to derive the greatest benefit from an orientation. A well-structured and well-paced program allows everyone to interact with colleagues, who may be grouped by discipline and seated at small tables. Brainstorming activities, especially in areas pertaining to teaching and learning, are beneficial in encouraging creative thinking and establishing a climate of shared issues. Such an approach also helps to create a sense of community among colleagues who may not otherwise see each other during the term, but who can now communicate via phone or e-mail.

Timing

Unlike incoming full-time faculty who usually are hired and start their duties in the fall, part-time faculty may have been away from an academic environment for some time, so an orientation session may be needed at a different time from the customary start of the fall semester. Multiple part-time faculty orientation sessions may be needed, depending on the school's calendar—whether it is run on the semester or the quarter system, for instance. In any case, the orientation should be held at least a month before the term begins. This is especially important for part-time faculty who are teaching for the very first time because it allows them time to develop their courses properly and thoughtfully, and for part-time faculty who are teaching for the first time at the particular school so they can make the necessary adjustments to policies, procedures, and requirements.

Online Orientations

There are many advantages to an online orientation for part-time faculty, such as continuous availability, ongoing updating, and time and space economies. However, if one of the major goals of an orientation is to create viable ties between part-time faculty and the school, an online orientation is no replacement for a face-to-face session. An online orientation can, nevertheless, serve as a supplement to a face-to-face program and as a ready source of information and updates. Some institutions have started constructing online new faculty orientation sites. Most, however, are simply online versions of a handbook.

Handbook

Regularly published faculty handbooks are mandated in many instances by the state or by governing boards and accrediting organizations. They contain prescribed and other important information and may become useful tools in resolving disputes. Yet, because part-time faculty are so often an invisible constituency, many important items of information go unpublished.

Should a separate part-time handbook be published? The answer depends on the quality and scope of the existing faculty handbook. If it can be expanded to include a special section relating to part-time faculty issues, or such issues can be integrated smoothly into various sections of the existing document, it would save valuable resources. On the other hand, if part-time faculty policies and practices have been developed in a systematic way and can be presented more clearly as a separate document, that's a viable option as well. One compelling reason for having a separate part-time faculty handbook is that it may also contain information for unit and department administrators about the hiring process and other matters that may not be included in the full-time faculty handbook.

A comprehensive part-time faculty handbook may contain the following sections and information:

1. Institutional Mission, Goals, and Values
2. Hiring/Firing/Employment Process and Policies
    - Identity of those authorized to hire part-time faculty
    - Position description development
    - Methods for broadcasting position availability
    - Application process—forms to be completed, deadlines, documentation, references
    - Selection process—review procedures, interview
    - Hiring process
    - Teaching loads
    - Pay procedures

- Supervision and performance review procedures—classroom observations, reports, etc.
- Job continuity
- Grounds for dismissal
- Dismissal process

3. Faculty Policies and Procedures
   - Student enrollment management issues—registration deadlines and proof of registration, add/drop policies, class rosters, grading deadlines, etc.
   - Administrative responsibilities of faculty—classroom assignments, record keeping, textbook ordering process, materials' duplication, keys and pass codes, mail, rules and regulations regarding permissible/nonpermissible classroom activities such as smoking, food, use of substitute instructors, etc.

4. A Guide to Campus Resource Organizations
   - Faculty support organizations—human resources, employee relations, health and wellness, equal opportunity, international exchange, parking, etc.
   - Student support organizations—learning center, disabilities office, new student orientation, commuter affairs, international students, graduate student affairs, etc.

5. Administrative Structure and Key Contacts Information
   - Organizational chart
   - Contact information for academic support—departments, library, audiovisual, technology resources, space assignment, bookstore, student registration, student records, etc.
   - Contact information for administrative support—campus security, campus closing information, office space, classroom and office keys, phone access, e-mail access, ID cards, etc.

6. Pedagogical Expectations
   - Syllabus preparation and availability
   - Attendance
   - Assignment standards
   - Required materials
   - Testing and assessment practices
   - Evaluation and grading policies

7. Performance Expectations
   - Office hours
   - Attendance at departmental meetings
   - Scheduling, including expected arrival time for class
   - Use of equipment
   - Clerical support availability
   - Confidentiality of student records
   - Copyright issues
   - Other responsibilities, such as student advising, scholarly activities, participation on committees, etc., when they are part of the expectations
8. Faculty Development Resources and Opportunities
9. Benefits Available to Part-time Faculty
10. Grievance Procedures
11. Statement of Institutional Standards
    - Academic freedom
    - Family educational rights and privacy act
    - Policy of nondiscrimination
    - Sexual harassment policy
    - Academic honesty/integrity
    - Honor code
12. Individual Department Addendum
    - Contact information
    - Guidelines regarding support services such as duplication, audiovisuals, administrative procedures, departmental meetings, etc.

Participation in Institutional Life

Part-time faculty's invisibility has the potential to deprive the school community of a valuable resource outside the classroom. Part-time faculty can bring not only their academic credentials and experience, but also the unique perspectives that full-time faculty and administrators may not possess. These include perspectives from the nonacademic world in which they may work—corporate, small business, government, and nonprofit organizations—as well as perspectives from other academic institutions at which they have worked.

Including part-time faculty in institutional life broadcasts the important message that they are a vital constituency and enriches discussion and programming. Some ways to formally integrate part-time faculty into aspects of institutional life include:

1. *Representation on the Faculty Senate* (or the main faculty governing organization). Such representation can be in a nonvoting status, and its benefits would derive from
   - Regular reports to the Senate about part-time faculty matters
   - Consultations on matters that may affect or be affected by part-time faculty involvement
   - Part-time faculty having their own voice on an institutional level
   - A setting for raising part-time faculty issues of which full-time faculty may not be aware
2. *Participation in Open Forums.* Part-time faculty can contribute valuable input and carry information back to their colleagues by participating in
   - Campuswide discussions
   - Planning activities
   - Preparation for accreditation—campuswide and within colleges
   - Faculty convocation
   - Graduation ceremonies
   - Short-term task forces
3. *Service on Committees.* Part-time faculty can be invited to serve on campuswide or college standing committees as well as special committees, including personnel committees that evaluate part-time faculty's performance. Such varied committees as those focused on uses of technology, curriculum development, approval of new courses, or student affairs can benefit greatly from part-time faculty input.
   - Awareness of policies and procedures. If part-time faculty representation is important for the reasons mentioned above, so, too, is strict adherence to institutional standards and their application across the board to all and by all who teach at the institution.
   - Academic freedom
     - The same coverage provided to full-time faculty needs to be ensured for part-time faculty.
     - Standards of academic freedom and academic conduct should

be consistent throughout the organization to ensure credibility in the eyes of internal and external constituencies.
- Grievance policies. Standards and procedures should be identical ("seamless") for part-time faculty and full-time faculty for identical activities. Student and/or faculty academic misconduct issues should be governed by a single set of regulations and procedures.

Access and Communication

An individual is connected to an organization in numerous ways, most of which are taken for granted. When one is a full-time employee of an academic institution, one's affiliation is so multifaceted that we seldom stop to ponder how the quality of performance would be affected if even a single connection were missing. For part-time faculty, most of these connections are generally missing.

Most of the suggestions made in this section involve minimal out-of-pocket expense for the institution; they do, however, offer direct and important ways for increasing connectivity with part-time faculty.

Phones

Most part-time faculty do not teach during "regular" school hours—they tend to teach during evenings, weekends, and early morning hours; they may also teach off campus in many instances. Lack of a campus phone means that communication with students, the department, and other campus offices has to be done via part-time faculty's personal phones. In addition to the cost involved for part-time faculty, their privacy is affected (and most are not paid for that time).

Access to a campus phone, therefore, is very important. While it may not be practical to assign separate equipment to each part-time instructor, a separate phone extension is important. Most large phone systems provide for a single central number to be used as access to numerous extensions (much as the main campus number provides). Individual extensions can also be equipped with voice mail capacity so that students can leave messages for their instructors, and conversely, instructors can leave messages for students. An added benefit of this approach is that such systems can be programmed so that departments and campus organizations can leave a single message through the single central number, which then can be broadcast to all or some of the part-time faculty at once.

E-mail

Increasingly, interoffice and schoolwide communication is done through e-mail messages, but because of the complexity of such systems, a local (campus) e-mail address is usually required. Most part-time faculty, if they have access to e-mail, tend to use commercial vendors for their service. The potential problems inherent in the use of such services—lack of compatibility, loss of contact when services are changed, restricted capacity, etc.—make it highly desirable that everyone associated with the institution, including part-time faculty, have a campus e-mail address. The system can be established as follows:

- Assign each part-time faculty, upon first employment, a campus e-mail address. The address can be indicated on the contract, or the part-time instructor can be required to find out the address through the usual channels.
- Provide an option for e-mail forwarding to the part-time faculty's private e-mail addresses so they do not need to check two separate e-mail systems.
- A "grace period" during which campus e-mail is still accessible is provided following employment termination, just as in the case of all other employees.
- The master list of all part-time faculty e-mail addresses can be used to broadcast important information such as professional development opportunities, special programs, etc.

Part-time Faculty Web Site

A special Web site, linked to the main institutional home page and dedicated to part-time faculty affairs, can be beneficial in several ways:

- It provides a central area for information important to part-time faculty.

- It provides access to information about part-time faculty affairs to the rest of the institutional community.
- It is a showcase of the institution's relationship with its part-time faculty that can be used for recruitment purposes.
- It provides for a ready access to necessary forms and changing information about policies and procedures.

Distribution Lists

Printed, electronic or other communications circulated by departments or campus organizations to full-time faculty, should be made available to part-time faculty as well. It not only shows a serious attempt to be inclusive, it also provides part-time faculty with important information they are not able to access on their own.

Where a regular staff/faculty newsletter is distributed across campus, a special section highlighting part-time faculty and their activities can be included. That is much more inclusive than a separate "part-time faculty bulletin."

ID Cards

A very simple means for indicating affiliation with the institution, an ID card can help when a part-time instructor who teaches at odd hours needs assistance from campus authorities. It is also useful in promoting participation in campus cultural and sports activities.

Parking

Part-time faculty may be employed for partial academic years—for single terms or even shorter periods. A reasonable arrangement would provide them with the option to purchase parking privileges, if there is a cost attached, for the period of employment only. Such prorated fees are consistent with prorated wages.

Library Privileges

Part-time faculty's teaching responsibilities are identical to those of full-time faculty, so they should have the same access to library resources, printed and electronic. With the increased use of online communication, it should be relatively simple to arrange for such library services as placing materials on reserve or scheduling special library-related (such as information literacy) instructional sessions to be done from remote locations so part-time faculty do not need to make extra trips to campus.

Use of Athletic Facilities

The same privileges extended to full-time faculty should be given to part-time faculty for use of any athletic or recreational facilities.

Faculty Club Membership

Where a faculty club exists, part-time faculty can be invited to join at a reduced rate. Such clubs are a great place for cross-departmental "mingling" and provide for professional networking and collegial activities.

Discounts

Any discounts offered to full-time faculty should also be available to part-timers. These may include bookstore discounts, discounts on tickets to campus cultural or sports events, cap-and-gown rental, or discounts for activities in the surrounding community.

Professional Development

All professional development opportunities generally available to full-time faculty, should be accessible to part-time faculty. The quality of teaching across the institution needs to be of uniform high quality. Until very recently, most full-time faculty were not specifically trained to teach at the college level. While some may have gained some experience and insights through work as graduate assistants, many others have not. Formally preparing graduate teaching assistants for college teaching is a relatively new phenomenon, so both full-time and part-time faculty likely could benefit from high-quality professional development programs. Furthermore, since both types of instructors may teach the same courses and the same students, it stands to reason that they have much to share with each other by way of experience, insights, and professional practice. Opportunities that consider part-time faculty as an integral constituency of the teaching community may include:

- Scheduling faculty development workshops and other activities at various times, not just during the day, so part-time faculty can participate—evenings and weekends are especially appropriate

- Providing information about research and grant opportunities— many of the same grants and fellowships available to full-time faculty are also available to part-time faculty. Unfortunately, these are not well publicized, so both part-time faculty and their departments are not aware of the possibilities. Some outstanding examples are listed in Connection 5.
- Participation in scholarly forums or other opportunities in which faculty share their scholarly activities and accomplishments
- Access to institutional funding sources for the improvement of teaching such as mini-grants or stipends
- Access to professional development opportunities for integrating technology into teaching and learning
- Invitation to submit original articles, reviews, and other scholarly materials to be included in institutional publications
- Access to funding, possibly prorated based on the proportion of the position, to attend external conferences and pedagogical seminars
- Tuition discounts for educational programs pursued at the institution—may include degree, certificate, and noncredit continuing education programs
- Inclusion in any reciprocal arrangements for continuing professional development at neighboring institutions

Recognition

An inclusive organization recognizes all of its members and celebrates the professional accomplishments of all of them. The mere mention of someone's employment by an academic institution can be perceived as a great honor. This may be important if recruitment and hiring of top-quality people is a goal—the outside community values education.

Recognition and acknowledgement can be accomplished in several ways, described below.

Catalogue Listings

Although not always permanent or long-term employees, part-time instructors are legitimate members of the faculty and should be listed in the catalogue and any other faculty lists, possibly after having taught for a predetermined period, such as a year or two. Students expect the same quality of teaching from part-time faculty as they do from full-time faculty, but they may question the quality of education they receive if their teachers' names appear nowhere in a formal setting.

In cases where the full-time instructor holds a full-time professional position elsewhere, that position could also be mentioned in the listing; it would have the added benefit of demonstrating to the community that the institution is part of the community.

Notice of Hiring

Local media are very receptive to news stories originating with an academic institution. An announcement of new part-time faculty hired for the upcoming term makes a nice story, especially if the faculty's professional background is described.

Similar announcements of hiring can be included in internal publications such as the monthly bulletin or online newsletter.

Achievement Awards

Many institutions recognize full-time faculty achievements in the three key areas of performance—teaching, scholarship/research, and service. If part-time faculty are truly involved in all three facets of academic life, their achievements should be recognized in all three. However, since teaching is the primary and most frequently the only activity part-time faculty are engaged in, the outline below recognizes outstanding achievements in teaching.

Full-time teaching awards are usually administered by the Faculty Senate or a similar faculty organization in collaboration with the administration. Since part-time faculty frequently are not members of such organizations, their excellence in teaching awards can be administered by the faculty development unit or by a similar unit within academic affairs. This sample program below has been administered at Florida International University since 1999.

Format and Process

- Nominations are solicited in early spring from full-time faculty, chairpersons, and deans. In addition to personal data, a nomination includes a one-page statement of the reasons for it.

- To be eligible, a part-time instructor must have taught at the institution for at least three years, two courses per year, counting fall, spring, and summer terms.
- Nominees are notified and invited to submit a portfolio demonstrating excellence in teaching. The portfolio includes
  - A resume or CV
  - A statement of the nominee's teaching philosophy
  - Three letters of reference: one from faculty, two from students
  - A list of courses taught, class size, and grade distribution
  - A syllabus of each course taught and a description of how the courses continued to improve over time
  - A list and samples of original materials created by the nominee
  - Student comments about the courses taught and any computer-tabulated standard student evaluations
- A selection committee made up of four to five full-time faculty from diverse disciplines reviews all portfolios and makes recommendations to the provost. The program has been structured so that all nominees are "winners" in that each one receives a plaque of Merit Recognition; several nominees whose achievements are noticeably above the rest may, if finances allow, receive a stipend.
- Part-time faculty teaching achievements are announced during the annual Faculty Convocation, at which full-time faculty are also recognized. This joint celebration of achievement helps the institutional community recognize not only the individual nominees, but also the important and equal role that part-timers can play in providing high-quality teaching.

Promotions

When part-time faculty are ranked in some fashion, either parallel to full-time faculty (i.e., assistant professor, associate professor, professor) or in their own unique way (i.e., junior instructor, senior instructor, etc.), any promotion can and should be broadcast in much the same way as that of full-time faculty, both internally and externally.

Notes

1. Elman, Sandra E. (2002, fall). Part-Time Faculty and Student Learning: A Regional Accreditation Perspective. *Peer Review, 5*(1), 16.

2. Longmate, Jack, and Cosco, Frank. (2002, May 3). Part-Time Instructors Deserve Equal Pay for Equal Work. *The Chronicle of Higher Education* (http://chronicle.com/weekly/v48/i34/34b01401.htm)

3. Statement from the Conference on the Growing Use of Part-Time and Adjunct Faculty. (1998, Jan./Feb.). *Bulletin of the American Association of University Professors, 84* (1).

TO THE DEPARTMENT

Steps in Developing a Collegial Community

Action Plans

The Challenge

The institution bears the major responsibility for the overall integration of part-time faculty, yet it is the individual department's responsibility to ensure the consistency and quality of programming. Institutional agendas and departmental goals, while parallel in the abstract sense, are usually divergent in the practical aspects of implementation. Departments are separate and semiautonomous cultural and professional entities, with their own sets of values and practices. Standards and practices often are informed more directly by outside accrediting and professional organizations than by internal institutional agendas. Part-time faculty are often caught in the middle of these conflicting interests. As the 1997 Statement from the Conference on the Growing Use of Part-Time and Adjunct Faculty suggests,

> The immediate cost savings that institutions realize from widespread use of part-time appointments to staff introductory courses are often offset by the lack of program coherence and reduced faculty involvement with students and student learning. The frequently inadequate facilities accessible to part-time faculty members, coupled with the inadequate professional support they often receive, create structural impediments that put even the most talented teachers at a severe disadvantage. The limited contractual and time commitments of part-time employment mean that temporary faculty members do their work apart from the structures through which the curriculum, department, and institution are sustained and renewed. Academic programs require high levels of permanent faculty involvement through department and college governance to maintain and renew curricula that offer students high-quality educational opportunities. . . . A heavy reliance on part-time faculty appointments . . . overburdens permanent faculty members with tasks . . . [related to]temporary faculty members who are disconnected from . . . these functions.[1]

Departments attempting to integrate part-time faculty face several key challenges. The first involves the natural tension between the desire to maintain a semiautonomous departmental culture while attempting to adhere to a set of institutional standards. The second challenge revolves around the need to create real and lasting connections among part-time faculty, full-time faculty, and departmental staff so departmental goals can be achieved most consistently and effectively. The third challenge is to create direct connections between part-time faculty and the educational processes of the department so students benefit from the best possible academic experience.

As the gateway to both the institution and the students, the department plays a pivotal role in both acclimating part-time faculty to the school and ensuring that they can perform at the highest level possible. By nature, academic departments function very much as standard places of work: the hours of operation are mostly traditional—early morning to late afternoon—and the administrative structure is top-down in nature with the chairperson as the head administrator, faculty as the professional staff, and office staff as support professionals. In contrast, many part-time faculty interact with the institution during unconventional hours—evenings and weekends, are not part of the departmental hierarchy, and have little or no contact with either full-time faculty or support staff.

It takes a large dose of determination, dedication, and just plain good planning to address the challenges and overcome some of the inherent obstacles. This section lays out action plans that can help a department become a more effective unit by integrating its part-time faculty and creating a unified professional entity.

Action Plans

Collegial Integration

Part-time and full-time faculty often seem to lead separate lives, their paths rarely crossing casually, let alone in purposeful ways. Divergent schedules, lack of information, and the absence of collaborative opportunities are only some of the reasons. Under these circumstances it is almost impossible to develop any kind of collegial relationships that can overcome the usual "us versus them" attitude.

Several activities and programmatic initiatives can help bridge the common distance between part-time faculty and the rest of the department:

Start-of-the-term Activities

Any departmental social activities at the start of the academic year should include part-time faculty. Additionally, because part-time faculty are usually employed on a term-by-term basis and a number of them may join the ranks in mid-year, a spring get-together may be beneficial.

Discussion Circles

Once or twice per term, informal discussion circles made up of part-time faculty as well as full-time faculty and other professional staff (such as lab technicians), can go a long way toward fostering collegial relations. The focus of such gatherings can be topical, can be for planning purposes, or can be just a social event. Since many part-time faculty hold other, full-time jobs elsewhere, an early breakfast or a light dinner away from campus may be an appropriate setting.

Informal Activities

Whenever the department, or a segment of it, engages in any informal activities such as monthly lunches in the faculty club, part-time faculty should be invited to join.

Common Practices

There are several ways by which part-time faculty can be apprised of departmental common practices:

- A mini-handbook focusing on nonacademic practices
- A Web site containing practical advice and appropriate links
- An occasional newsletter/bulletin put together by faculty (of all ranks) for faculty

Recognition

Private and public expressions of gratitude for contributions made to the welfare of the department and its students go a long way toward fostering camaraderie and goodwill. Such recognition need not involve extraordinary accomplishments; rather, it should be for a job well done.

Highlighting the Part-time Faculty

At either informal occasions, such as those listed above, or formal occasions, such as workshops and departmental meetings, part-time faculty can be invited to make presentations about their professional activities. Of special interest are presentations that tie together academic content and the part-time faculty's experiences outside of academe.

Professional Integration

To maintain standards of quality and consistency, all who work for the department, and especially those who teach, need to work as a unit. While individual approaches and interests are certainly a cornerstone of academic departments and should be promoted, some agreement about common practices serves as the basis for a well-functioning department. It is especially critical when both full-time and part-time faculty teach sections of a single course, and when courses are part of a sequence. In both cases, ongoing communication, starting with the process of curriculum development and learning objectives definition, and continuing through course implementation and quality/learning assessment, is essential to the integrity of the academic program and to student satisfaction. Activities that help promote professional integration of part-time faculty, while somewhat similar to institutional initiatives, nevertheless are essential on the departmental level, as the following items suggest.

Recruitment and Hiring

As is the case with full-time faculty recruitment and hiring, members of the department should be involved in recruiting and hiring part-time faculty. They should help define needs, assignments, and qualifications; suggest recruitment venues and participate in active recruitment; assist in developing screening and hiring procedures; and serve on selection committees.

Orientation to the Department

In addition to the institutional part-time faculty orientation, a departmental orientation, much shorter in duration, can help professional integration from the very start of employment. The chairperson and some full-time and veteran part-time faculty should be involved in planning and conducting such orientations. Full-time faculty can participate on a rotating basis if the department is very large; otherwise, everyone should at least be introduced.

Policies and Procedures

Departmental ways of conducting business need to be organized and published in easy reference format. Due to part-time faculty's scattered schedule of teaching, they need to be able to access important information easily and quickly. Printed materials are adequate; Web sites are better in that information can be updated easily and in a timely manner, and access is more readily available.

Access to Information

Much important information is circulated through departments informally because most full-time faculty are physically present at predictable times. Reports, notices of special programs or opportunities, and similar announcements have to be readily available to part-time faculty.

Curriculum Development

Professionalism starts with being part of the development process. To truly "own" a course, the teacher needs to be involved in its development to some degree. Part-time faculty, all of them in small departments or their representatives in larger departments, should be invited to participate in curriculum development and evaluation activities. Not only will they benefit from such participation, but the department will gain from their insights and experience as well.

Textbook/Materials Selection

Departments vary in their approaches to textbook selection. Some prescribe a single text or set of materials, others leave the choice entirely to the individual instructor, and still others create a pool of approved materials from which individual instructors can select. While there are advantages and disadvantages to any of these approaches, all would benefit from part-time faculty's input into the selection and evaluation processes.

Departmental Meetings

Full-time faculty's schedule dictates that departmental meetings be held during the day. It would benefit both the department and its part-time faculty if at least some of these meetings were held at "off" hours such as late after-noons before evening classes start or early mornings. So much essential pro-fessional activity takes place during departmental meetings that excluding part-time faculty is both noncollegial and counterproductive. Similar to all departmental activities, part-time faculty's participation in and contribution to regular meetings can improve departmental performance.

Committee Work

Part-time faculty can and should be invited to become involved with the work of departmental committees. Their participation can be in proportion to their numbers on the faculty, or they can be asked to choose a representa-tive. In some cases they may be voting members, in others they may serve in an ex-officio capacity.

Access to Chairperson

Professional guidance is important in all cases, and especially in the case of part-time faculty who interface with the institution at odd times. The chair-person can hold office hours to meet with part-time faculty, and such office hours can be scheduled on a rotating basis during evening hours on days that part-time faculty teach. Those who teach on weekends can also take advan-tage of evening office hours.

Performance Evaluation

The process and standards for part-time faculty's performance should be completely consistent with those of full-time faculty, even though the scope of their activity may focus mostly on teaching. Goals for the term/year should be articulated, standards of performance defined, an evaluation pro-cess agreed upon, and timely and constructive feedback provided. It is espe-cially important to avoid the temptation of using end-of-course student evaluations as the sole evaluative criterion of part-time faculty's performance. First, because such evaluations tend to be limited in scope, and second, be-cause coming as they do at the end of the course, they leave no room for adjustments and improvements. Too often, reliance on student evaluations (which are sometimes viewed as popularity contests) as the sole performance indicator may lead to more relaxed grading standards if instructors perceive the likelihood of continued employment as tied to student evaluations.

Respect for Time Constraints

Many part-time faculty lead varied professional lives and have limited time available for nonessential activities. If they are to be included in departmental activities such as meetings and committee deliberations, every effort should be made to ensure that time is well organized. Efficient meeting management, for instance, can be beneficial (and appreciated by full-time faculty as well): shorter meetings, a well-organized agenda published before the meeting, punctuality and promptness, and focused, timed discussion are some ingredients of a well-run meeting.

Access to Technology

Opportunities for training and using technology in professional activities such as instruction and its preparation (research) need to be available to part-time faculty. Whether these opportunities are scheduled as a single, intensive workshop; made available through online tutorials; or provided in varying time slots, they must reflect sensitivity to the availability of part-time faculty.

Coordination

When there are more than a handful of part-time faculty in a department, it is prudent to assign a coordinator who can focus on ensuring that all matters pertaining to part-time faculty are handled well. While the departmental secretary may handle some coordinating activities capably, others may call for more specialized handling. One possible approach is to assign part-time faculty coordination tasks to a full-time faculty member on a rotating annual basis. In exchange, that person will be released from part of his or her teaching duties. Some of the coordinator's activities may include the following:

- Coordinating recruitment and selection of part-time faculty
- Liaison to campus services when part-time faculty cannot make contact themselves—pick up audio visual equipment, deliver grading information and student evaluations, etc.
- Ordering textbooks
- Collecting course syllabi
- Distributing class rosters
- Arranging for classroom, lab, and technology access

- Providing office space, storage space (filing cabinets, bookcase), keys, etc.
- Troubleshooting
- Classroom observations and feedback
- Facilitating communication

Access and Communication

Full-time faculty take for granted much of the support needed for quality teaching simply because they are present during regular operating hours. Part-time faculty who teach at uncommon times cannot casually assume such support. In many instances departmental support staff tend to ignore part-time faculty's needs simply because those faculty are invisible or because the department has not developed mechanisms for accommodating their needs. For a well-functioning department, the following items of access and communication are needed:

- *Secretarial support.* Whatever assistance secretaries and other office personnel provide to full-time faculty, the same assistance should be provided to part-time faculty, and just as cheerfully. A method for communicating needs, sufficient lead time, and ways to access materials at off hours, all need to be spelled out as a consistent process.
- *Classroom assignments and access.* Part-time faculty may not have an opportunity to preview classrooms, ascertain their suitability, or check for size and conditions. All of these need to be done by someone, either a secretary or part-time faculty coordinator, in consultation with individual part-time instructors.
- *Office space.* Physical connection to the department and its members is an important element of a well-functioning unit. It may be impractical to expect that each part-time instructor will have a separate office, so other arrangements can be made, such as:
  - Shared space in which several part-time faculty have desks, bookshelves, and filing cabinets
  - Rotating space used by different part-time instructors at different times of day and on different days

  Meeting students during office hours, sharing information with colleagues, and interfacing with administrative staff are all part of being a college instructor, and a base of operations in the form of a desk and/or part of an office within the department is certainly preferable to a coffee table in the cafeteria or a bench between buildings.

- *Phone and e-mail access.* Each part-time instructor should have an institutional phone extension number along with voicemail capabilities as well as an institutional e-mail address.
- *E-mail address.* This information should be published and posted in the same manner as for full-time faculty and staff, including in the school's printed directory, online staff directory, and central phone operator's ("information") data.
- *Mail and announcement distribution.* Part-time faculty should receive their mail, including institutional and departmental announcements and materials, regularly. A secure location outside the department's main office (which may need to be securely locked at off hours) can be established, and access by way of a key or pass card provided to each part-time instructor.
- *Materials duplication.* Unless the part-time instructor has access to a copying machine at another place of work, the department should provide such access. If materials are to be duplicated by office staff, procedures for submitting requests and delivering materials need to be established and publicized. Policies and procedures in this area should be consistent for all faculty; however, if duplication is handled within the department, a separate drop-off and/or pickup location needs to be established for those not on the premises during regular working hours. Other alternatives include creating a charge account at a campus or neighboring copying service or providing copy cards that can be used at campus duplicating machines. Reimbursements for copying expenses incurred by part-time faculty are also possible, but they tend to be cumbersome.

Mentoring

There is no stronger and more effective way to connect to and integrate into a department's life than to have part-time faculty pair up with full-time faculty in a mentoring relationship. Although sometimes involving several individuals in a mentoring "circle," mentoring is usually a one-on-one strategy that is by far the most effective and most inclusive arrangement possible. Mentoring is a two-way relationship marked by confidentiality, mutual support, openness, and friendliness.

The goals and benefits of a departmental mentoring program for part-time faculty are:

- Induction of new hires into the institutional and departmental culture
- Promotion of professional development
- Promotion of retention of the best part-time faculty
- Increased collegiality
- Increased interaction between part-time and full-time faculty on matters important to both such as curriculum development and classroom management
- Promotion of teaching and learning enhancement
- Improved channels of communication

Rather than creating a narrow focus for the mentoring relationship, successful programs realize that to attain the greatest benefits from the program, for individuals as well as departments, the scope of topics and activities needs to be flexible and be allowed to include personal and social matters as well as professional ones. The professional effectiveness of an individual is not achieved in isolation from the rest of the person's life, and a nurturing mentoring relationship recognizes this fact and capitalizes on it. An interesting example is the mentoring program at Lesley University.[2]

Program Origination and Structure

A mentoring program can originate with administrators or interested faculty can start one. It can include everyone in the department, or it can involve a few at a time, rotating to include everyone over time. The number of full- and part-time faculty, and administrative logistics, dictate how the program evolves and operates. It is important to remember that one of the goals of a mentoring program for part-time faculty is to increase retention; it stands to reason, therefore, that over time, the number of "new" part-time faculty may decrease, as could the scope of the program. The model suggested here differs from other mentoring programs, however, in that it is not intended to be just an "initiation" program to break new recruits into the department by mentoring them for a semester or two. Rather, it is suggested that an ongoing mentoring relationship in which an individual part-time instructor may be paired with a succession of mentors over an indefinite period could best achieve the goals stated above. Part-time faculty, after all, are not physically present for many of the department's informal and formal activities, so their ongoing close relationship with at least one full-time faculty is a sure way to bridge some of the spatial and temporal gaps.

When a mentoring program has been established, an orientation session for both mentors and mentored is essential. This can be done for a pair of faculty (mentor and mentored) or for a larger group. The orientation's purposes are:

- To define the program's goals and objectives
- To suggest formats for pairs to develop
- To provide information about effective (nonjudgmental) listening skills, feedback skills, and goal-setting methods

Duration of a Mentoring Relationship

Ideally, a mentoring relationship should be established for a minimum of one academic year at a time. Some part-time faculty may teach irregularly, skipping a spring semester for instance, but if they are to be long-term employees, they need an ongoing connection to the department. During "off" semesters, increased online and phone communication between mentor and mentored can replace face-to-face meetings.

Rotating mentors, as mentioned earlier, is important in exposing part-time faculty to multiple points of view, approaches, and practices.

Selection of Mentors

As in all instances of trying to match two individuals, the selection of mentors and the assignment of mentored part-time faculty can depend on many variables—age, academic interest, gender, etc. A case can be made for matching individuals with similar traits, and just as strong a case can be made for matching individuals with dissimilar traits. Whatever the criteria used, flexibility is key. Keeping in mind the goals of the mentoring program, pairing decisions can be made for a variety of reasons, and the recommended rotation approach can ensure that the rarely occurring poor match need not be permanent.

Typical Issues Addressed in a Mentoring Relationship

- Departmental policies and procedures
  - Becoming familiar with processes involved in performing duties—classroom assignments, textbook selection and ordering, technology use, etc.

- ▪ Understanding relationships, responsibilities, expectations
- ▪ Becoming familiar with administrative forms and reports
- Growth as a teacher
- Developing skills
- Understanding how learning is evaluated
- Understanding how teaching is evaluated
- Receiving feedback about teaching
- Recognizing the relationship between teaching and learning, between teachers and students
- Understanding institutional and departmental standards related to the performance of duties such as testing, grading, interaction with students, etc.
- Familiarity with faculty and student support organizations
- Growth as a member of the community
- Developing relationships within the department
- Understanding institutional culture
- Developing relationships outside the department
- Growth as a professional
- Discovering opportunities for research and other scholarly activities
- Networking with others in the field, outside the institution

Format

For a mentoring relationship to be productive and successful, it should have few constraints. As in all relationships, mentoring happens in many and varied ways, most of them unstructured. Mentors and mentored should be able to develop their own format and style; however, some activities are expected of every mentoring team:

- Visits to each other's classes and follow-up meetings for feedback
- A minimum number of scheduled meetings—place, time, duration, and topics of discussion to be left to the participants
- Attendance at programs specifically designed for mentoring program participants such as professional presentations, Q&A with key administrators, and social gatherings

Possible Roles of the Mentor

- Transmit organizational information.
- Help interpret policies, procedures, and standards.

- Explain the governance system.
- Assist in setting goals and monitoring progress toward achieving them.
- Coach in specific skills and competencies.
- Provide support.
- Be a role model.
- Observe, listen, and provide constructive feedback.
- Assist in identifying and making networking connections.
- Serve as a professional colleague.

Possible Expectations of the Mentored

- Communicate openly with the mentor.
- Be open to receiving constructive feedback.
- Set realistic goals.
- Be flexible.
- Act on new information provided by the mentor.

Recognition

For both the mentor and the mentored, this critical activity should be considered "service" to the department and the institution at the highest possible level. Notes of appreciation from the department's chairperson and similar information placed in the personnel files are appropriate.

Since a mentoring program may be started at the departmental level and not originate as an institution-wide initiative, publicity is important and instructive. A list of participants in a short "thank you" note or report in the school's newsletter or as an e-mail message circulated to the entire faculty can help promote the concept and will certainly expand understanding of the possibilities.

Notes

1. Statement from the Conference on the Growing Use of Part-Time and Adjunct Faculty. (1998, Jan./Feb.). *Bulletin of the American Association of University Professors, 84* (1).

2. Ziegler, Carol A., and Reiff, Marianne. (2006, May). Adjunct Mentoring, a Vital Responsibility in a Changing Educational Climate: The Lesley University Adjunct Mentoring Program. *Mentoring & Tutoring, 14* (2), 247–269.

CONNECTION 3

TO TEACHING

Steps in Enhancing a Culture of Quality Teaching

Action Plans

The Challenge

There seems to be a widespread assumption that part-time faculty are less prepared for teaching than are full-time faculty. The reality is that neither group has been trained to teach; faculty members of all varieties have been trained in their specific fields and disciplines—history, biology, math, or business. Some full-time and part-time faculty who were fortunate enough to serve as graduate teaching assistants may have had some hands-on preparation for teaching that others have not. It is only recently that "preparing future faculty" programs have started appearing sporadically across the country. For the vast majority of faculty, their first day in the first classroom is also their first teaching experience. In that regard, full-time and part-time faculty are alike. As Gappa and Leslie point out,

> Although our interviewees had little hard evidence about differences in the quality of classroom performance between full- and part-time faculty, deans and department chairs . . . almost uniformly agreed that they could observe no practical difference on the average. To the extent that we could get people to suggest any distinction at all, some responded that the range of teaching performance might be slightly greater among the part-timers, with some cases of outstanding teaching and perhaps a few more problem cases.[1]

Where full-time faculty sometimes have an advantage is in the scope of their experience as teachers—by virtue of having taught longer or more courses, they have become more familiar with the issues and with prevailing practices. This kind of familiarity, by itself, is no guarantee of more effective teaching.

Having said that, part-time faculty do face challenges that may be unique to their function:

- They are not immersed in the ongoing, informal discussion of teaching and learning that takes place among full-time faculty.
- They may be less likely to experiment with new approaches and methodologies, especially if their teaching is a part-time addendum to a full-time job elsewhere.

- They are more likely to stick to a simple teaching formula, lecture style mostly, that, because they lack formal training, provides them with a relative "comfort zone."
- They may prefer to use the corporate training model of instruction over the academic teaching model, simply because it is more familiar and they are more comfortable with it.
- They may tend to be able to integrate "real world" experiences and applications into theoretical teaching, especially if they themselves are practicing professionals in the field.
- They may be willing and able to integrate workplace skills into coursework, especially when such integration is pointed out as beneficial—after all, they know firsthand the value of such skills.
- They may not have incentives to understand and fully implement long-term educational goals of the department and/or the institution.
- They may feel left out of the governance process and therefore exposed in areas such as academic freedom. This may lead to self-censoring in the process of teaching, including a very careful and limited choice of assignments and extensive, sometimes exclusive, use of multiple-choice tests.
- They may tend to minimize assignments to reduce out-of-classroom (unpaid) workload.

An often overlooked challenge has to do with finding ways to take advantage of part-time faculty's special skills and experiences for the benefit of the whole department or institution. Many part-time faculty bring a unique perspective in both content area and broader view of the discipline. In other instances, part-time faculty's world experience with application of the subject matter effectively complements full-time faculty's expertise in theory and research. Finding ways to integrate both strengths to the benefit of the students is a challenge worth pursuing.

Action Plans

Participation in Teaching and Learning Development Activities

To increase the likelihood that teaching and learning will occur at the highest possible levels, both teacher and students have to be engaged in the process.

For the teacher, such engagement has to take place at two different but connected times: first, during development of the course, and, second, while teaching the course. The two processes are related. The former is discussed in this section, the latter is discussed in Connection 4.

Engagement of part-time faculty in the course development process requires getting away from the practice of handing instructors a textbook, a class roster, and a piece of chalk and sending them into the classroom. That old notion of "preparation" for teaching is a recipe for developing instructors who are disengaged from the process, less than optimal teaching and learning levels, and dissatisfaction of all involved.

Below are suggestions for engaging part-time faculty in teaching and learning development activities.

Curriculum Development

Obviously, not all part-time faculty can be engaged in the ongoing process of academic program and curriculum development on either the departmental or the institutional level—not any more than all full-time faculty members are engaged in this important undertaking. Part-time faculty's engagement in the process can be encouraged by asking for volunteers who have an interest in the area to be part of the group (committee) that works on curricular issues, or by having part-time faculty select representatives who rotate in the role. One of the critical missing links in part-time faculty's frame of reference is an understanding of how individual courses fit within the larger academic picture. Participation by part-time faculty in discussions about developing, maintaining, or modifying curricula is important for their own performance as well as for their full-time colleagues, who may be exposed to new and maybe surprising points of view.

An important part of program and curriculum development is identifying learning objectives—what students will know or be able to do as a result of completing the program or any of its components. Tied to this, of course, is the need to identify and develop evaluative processes that will demonstrate whether learning goals are being met and, if so, how well they are met. Direct involvement by part-time faculty in this process certainly promotes a deeper understanding of the expectations associated with their teaching.

New Course Development

Part-time faculty who have taught at the same department for a while can be invited to develop new courses consistent with departmental curriculum planning. These courses could be new to the department, in which case teaming up part-time and full-time faculty may be smart and productive. Course development may also involve restructuring existing courses already taught by part-time faculty. As instruction moves further into Web-assisted, hybrid, and distance-learning formats, modification of both content and pedagogies is essential. This could be especially attractive to part-time faculty in that these formats require less reliance on fixed schedules and restricted locations for teaching and learning.

Textbook and Resource Selection

Departmental practices in the matter of textbook adoption by part-time faculty have run the full gamut, from the most restrictive model in which one textbook is used by all, to a total lack of cohesiveness in which each of numerous part-time faculty in the department chooses a different textbook. Since part-time faculty tend to teach many introductory courses, some agreement on textbooks and other instructional resources is prudent and practical. Faculty teaching succeeding levels expect a certain degree of consistent proficiency from students enrolling in their courses. On the other hand, limiting instruction by all faculty members to a single textbook may not expose instructors and students to diverse approaches and opportunities. Therefore, this important departmental discussion of textbook selection should include part-time faculty.

Similarly, part-time faculty should be involved in discussion of library resource selection, both print and electronic. Many college/university libraries consult with the disciplines about the choice of periodical subscriptions, purchase of reference materials, and access to electronic journals and other resources. For libraries to meet departmental and individual disciplines' needs, faculty input is essential, and part-time faculty should be part of such input.

Grading Standards

While usually left to the discretion of individual instructors, grading standards are a matter for departmental and institutional discussion and agreement. Full-time faculty members have numerous informal opportunities to discuss such matters and to compare practices; part-time faculty are usually left out of these discussions. It is important to remember that many part-time faculty are practicing professionals in their fields and are used to a performance evaluation system very different from academic grading. Such a system, while it does not necessarily assign numerical value to performance, does rate individuals' achievement based on "what they can do" rather than "what they know." Involving part-time faculty in formal or semiformal discussions of grading standards would benefit the whole program.

Teaching Enhancement

Too often, part-time and full-time faculty are separated when it comes to teaching development activities such as workshops, seminars, brown-bag discussion groups, and the like. Such segregation is counterproductive and is usually based on the assumption that there is great disparity in the quality of teaching between the two groups. Teaching development activities conducted jointly for part-time and full-time faculty (and sometimes including graduate teaching assistants, when appropriate) offer several important advantages:

- They provide an opportunity for individuals to learn from each other, regardless of their status.
- They help foster informal connections between part-time and full-time faculty in their own departments (if the program is department-based) and in other departments (if the program allows for open enrollment).
- They promote collegiality and a sense of "we are all in this together."
- They are financially sound in that they avoid unnecessary duplication.

Types of teaching enhancement activities include workshops and discussion groups. Department-based or open enrollment sessions focus on the following and on areas related to them.

Workshops

Pedagogy
- Course development
- Syllabus development
- Assignment development
- Learning styles
- Teaching styles
- Assessment of learning

- Testing options
- Teaching large classes
- Teaching adults and mixed-age groups
- Academic courses and corporate training—similarities/differences and course adaptations that take advantage of the best of both approaches
- Specific approaches such as problem-based learning, service learning, etc.

Technology-enhanced Teaching and Learning

- Computer skills
- Course content development and adjustment for the online environment
- Communication in the online environment
- Course management systems such as WebCT and Blackboard

Information Literacy—Research in the New Information Environment

- Navigating the new information environment
- Information literacy standards (by accrediting organizations) and their application in the teaching/learning environment
- Course and assignment adaptations and enhancements

Discussion Groups

Discussion groups provide opportunities for part-time and full-time faculty who teach identical or related courses to meet periodically to compare notes, share insights and new resources, consider shared projects such as service learning opportunities and field trips, and address any other topics that people who are engaged in similar activities can benefit from discussing.

Relations with Teaching Support Organization

Placing print or electronic resources on reserve in the library or identifying the most appropriate audiovisual equipment for the support of teaching and learning are common issues instructors face. Similarly, many full-time faculty take for granted support services for students with disabilities, writing and English-as-a-second-language (ESL) services, or student psychological counseling services. Part-time faculty may teach away from the main campus and on odd days and at off hours, so they may not have easy access to these and similar support systems and tend, therefore, to avoid using them. Access and use, and consequently, teaching can be enhanced significantly by any of the following approaches:

- Ensure that support services are available directly or remotely (online) at all hours during which, and all locations where, courses are offered.
- Ensure that key support personnel, such as the reserve or reference librarians, provide part-time faculty with current information about their services.
- Assign a departmental liaison to the service organizations to advocate for part-time faculty, especially in departments employing a large number of them.
- Where the resource organizations themselves, such as the library, have librarians assigned as liaisons to specific discipline areas, ensure that they are aware of and communicate with the part-time faculty in these units.

Online Resources for Teaching and Learning Enhancement

Nowadays there is a significant amount of comprehensive and useful teaching and learning information online. Some key sites and gateways are listed here:

- Online Faculty Teaching Excellence Network (OFTEN)
  http://inst.sfcc.edu/~often/index.htm
- 4faculty—resources developed by the California Community College System
  www.4faculty.org
- The Teaching and Learning Center (TLC) at the University of Nevada, Las Vegas
  http://tlc.unlv.edu
- Master lists of institutional online teaching and learning centers' Web sites
  http://www.hofstra.edu.faculty/ctse/cte_inks.cfm

Teaching Certificate Programs

Much has been stated so far about the need to develop inclusive environments in which part-time faculty become an integral part of the institution and the department. The teaching certificate program for part-time faculty described in this section, while appearing to contradict this approach, is in reality another way of creating connections between part-time faculty and the institution, and for broadcasting to the internal and external communities that part-time faculty are valued as professionals. Furthermore, developed as a free, voluntary program, this approach provides part-time faculty with an opportunity to demonstrate their commitment to teaching and to the institution.

Part-time faculty certificate programs have existed for a while, mostly in community colleges. In many of these instances, the programs revolve primarily around administrative matters—rules and regulations, standards, processes, etc. In some instances, they include an introductory pedagogy course/workshop designed exclusively for part-time faculty. Such programs provide a good start and could be expanded, as suggested below. The following model was developed and successfully implemented at Florida International University. It is cost effective in that it primarily uses services and programs already in existence, and it is programmatically effective in that it helps promote, at the departmental and institutional levels, discussion of high-quality teaching and learning. Its success, by the way, flies in the face of the frequent comment that part-time faculty will not choose to engage in "extra" activities that do not involve extra financial compensation.

Program Overview

The purpose of the part-time faculty teaching certificate program is to provide opportunities for enhancing teaching skills at the college/adult level. While most college-level instructors are experts in their specific disciplines, few have had any formal training in teaching, and while practical experience is extremely valuable, the teaching repertoire is usually limited to one's own exposure as a student.

The program is voluntary, free of charge, and can be completed at the participants' own pace. Participants enroll directly or can be referred by the department.

The program is administered centrally through the faculty development center, and it taps into the same resources used for all of its programs, including those for full-time faculty.

Program Requirements

The program contains several required and several self-selected activities that can be completed in any sequence. Requirements include:

- Attendance at an intensive introduction to teaching workshop
- Attendance at a minimum of six faculty development workshops or forums on campus. Rarely, and only under special circumstances, are workshops attended at other institutions acceptable. This limitation is consistent with the goal of promoting interaction between full-time and part-time faculty.
- Maintain and turn in a reflective journal of teaching for two courses taught during consecutive semesters. This requirement may be modified to allow for a "skipped" semester to conform to hiring patterns. The journal includes session planning notes, session evaluations—what went well, what didn't, and how it will be addressed in the future, and a reflection on the entire session. The journal is turned in as part of a course portfolio that also includes a reflective summary of the whole semester's teaching experience, the syllabus, any handouts developed by the instructor, student feedback, and grade distribution. Journals are reviewed and returned before the start of the following semester, so any feedback can be incorporated into planning and teaching the next course.
- Short reviews of three scholarly articles focused on pedagogy in the participant's disciplines
- A three- to four-page written statement of one's personal views on teaching
- Completion of any special requirements established by the participant's department such as attending a workshop on the use of graphing calculators in the mathematics department or a departmental lecture by a visiting scholar in history
- A written acknowledgment by the department chairperson of the participant's involvement in and completion of the requirements for the certificate program. The reasons why individual part-time faculty participate in a certificate program and why departments are interested in them vary. They can be summarized as

- A desire for professional enhancement, especially in an area (teaching) that may not be one's primary occupation
- An opportunity to complete an academic-based program that carries some weight in nonacademic work environments
- A way to develop relationships with other part-time faculty and with full-time faculty
- A way to build a differentiated part-time faculty pay scale based on quality and commitment
- A way to develop seniority among part-time faculty in teaching assignments and other departmental activities

Assessment

Evaluation of teaching is a complex and often politically charged issue. In too many instances the sole method for evaluating the effectiveness of teaching is a short document, a "student evaluation," administered at the end of the semester. Sometimes state or other external agencies mandate use of the form and its format. Many of the items students are asked to address involve course management matters rather than substantive teaching and learning issues. While such forms are used equally for courses taught by part-time and full-time faculty, some anecdotal data suggest that there is a major distinction in the perception of the function of these forms. It revolves around the fact that part-time faculty are usually hired for a single semester at a time, so the student evaluation form may serve as the only criterion for contract renewal or denial. The result, too often, is that part-time faculty, aware that their continued employment may hinge on the students' evaluations, tend to relax their standards to influence student responses. While "grade inflation" may be too strong a term to use, there could be concern about the relationship between evaluation modes and grading standards.

As in all teaching situations, depending on a single feedback mechanism, especially one that is administered at the end of the process, is not a very productive or useful approach. Foster and Foster observed that part-time faculty (and graduate students) are rarely evaluated or mentored by other faculty members. They are primarily evaluated by students, increasing the possibility that students will pressure them for better grades. In addition, this kind of limited and student-focused evaluation may cause part-time faculty to avoid teaching controversial topics or to confront instances of academic misconduct.[2]

None of the evaluation processes suggested below are, or should be, exclusive to part-time faculty. Too often some of these are available to full-time but not to part-time faculty. If a department sees itself as a single cohesive teaching unit interested in attaining and sustaining the highest possible quality, these processes should be universal.

Assessment standards and processes as they apply to teaching and learning should be developed jointly by full- and part-time faculty and universally understood. Teaching and learning assessment outcomes, when derived in multiple formats and based on substantive issues rather than superficial ones, should become an important component (but not the only one) in determining seniority for assignments, promotions, and other personnel decisions. Methods for assessment of the quality of teaching include those listed below.

Peer Evaluation in Which Colleagues Evaluate Each Other's Teaching

Rationale

- Conversations among peers about teaching and learning as a professional undertaking place teaching center-stage as a valued activity.
- Peer review provides faculty with a high degree of control over their work performance as teachers.
- Peer review allows faculty, rather than administrators, to play a major role in defining and assessing "quality teaching and learning."

Purposes

- To help colleagues enhance their teaching
- To help oneself enhance teaching
- To develop meaningful information for performance reviews
- To create a collegial dialogue about teaching and learning
- To help faculty and department agree on meaningful and measurable standards of teaching performance
- To ascertain that departmental goals and desired outcomes are pursued consistently
- To foster an environment in which high-quality teaching is a regular and frequent topic of conversation
- To reduce or remove any punitive aspects of performance assessment

- To establish standards for and observations of potential faculty preparation for teaching

Strategies

- Syllabus discussion is a regular, periodic activity to ensure that courses are well aligned with departmental goals and to provide opportunities for sharing teaching approaches and methods.
- Course material review takes a close look at textbooks, Web sources, and supplementary readings and materials.
- Teaching portfolios—see expanded, separate discussion below.
- Classroom observation provides a well-structured and planned opportunity for colleagues to visit each other's classrooms. It is a triple-step approach that includes (1) a preview in which the instructor to be visited outlines the planned session and approaches, (2) the visit, and (3) a follow-up discussion of what was observed and ideas for enhancement. For a good understanding of the specific course environment, it is advisable that more than one observation be conducted per semester, and that different individuals do the observing.
- Mentoring—see discussion in Connection 2.
- Micro-teaching allows individual faculty members to take turns presenting to the rest of the faculty—or to a select group—a capsule (mini) version of a course or session. Discussion and questions are included.
- Videotaping allows each faculty member to videotape a session or more of a course, which can be viewed and reviewed by other faculty members.
- Reflective journal of teaching contains information that includes plans for each session, evaluation of what worked well and what didn't, and thoughts about future adjustments.
- Resource banks house shared resources such as syllabi, student projects, and other materials for each course; they are stored centrally and are available to all faculty members for review.

Teaching Portfolios

Teaching portfolios are an excellent mechanism for documenting and continuously assessing teaching. Similar to artists' portfolios, they contain a variety of documentation and materials that demonstrate the instructor's capabilities and achievements. A separate portfolio may be kept for each course taught, or one may be developed as a long-range document, encompassing several parallel courses or a number of courses over a period of time. Typically, a teaching portfolio includes

- A statement of teaching philosophy, either for the individual course or as a general professional statement
- Syllabi
- Sample assignments
- Evaluative criteria used by the instructor—the indicators that are assessed for quality and what value or relative value is assigned to each of them. An example would be "ability to state clearly a hypothesis" or "demonstration of the process followed in determining the outcome."
- Resources used and the selection process involved
- Original materials developed by the instructor
- Ongoing student feedback
- Sample student work

Continuous Learning Assessment

Waiting for the end of the semester to find out whether teaching was effective, or what students perceive about their own learning, is not a very effective way to gauge quality. It is analogous to assigning a term paper that is to be turned in the last week of the semester, without any feedback from the instructor during its preparation. Any evaluation of such a paper is meaningless in that the course is over, and neither improvement nor additional learning can take place.

What is useful, then, is a way to assess teaching and learning as an ongoing process during the entire semester. The two methods suggested here can be used separately or simultaneously.

Two-minute Feedback

At the conclusion of a class session, unit of study, or any other short-term period, students are asked to write on a piece of paper a one-sentence response to each of the following three questions:

- What was the most important element or information obtained during this session/unit/week? (For a unit or longer period, multiple items may be asked for.)

- What one new thing did you learn?
- For what part of this session/unit would you like to have further discussion or clarification?

The effectiveness of this approach is in its simplicity and timeliness. Within minutes, the instructor is able to gauge whether most students were able to identify the most important part of the lesson. Also evident are those parts that need further clarification, an important factor in pacing a class. Finally, the students become aware of what they are actually learning.

Student Perceptions of Learning

In this approach, the instructor identifies a dozen or so desired learning outcomes students are expected to accomplish during the course. The list is given to students at the start of the semester as part of the course introduction. At a couple of key junctures during the semester and once near its end, students are asked to rate the degree to which they feel they have learned each of the items on the list. They can respond to cues such as, "I feel I have mastered this," "I have some familiarity with it but need further study," "I have a vague idea about this," and "I have no idea what this is."

This approach is valuable in assessing not only content areas but also key skill areas such as research abilities, teamwork, critical thinking, etc.

Recognition

The need for recognition of part-time faculty's efforts and accomplishments has been mentioned previously as one way to integrate part-time faculty into institutional and departmental life. In the context of teaching, however, recognition is even more significant. For most part-time faculty, teaching is the only specific activity they are engaged in within the department and the institution, and their self-worth and professional reputation and success are riding on its successful execution. Feedback about their teaching and recognition of achievements in that arena are, therefore, critical. While not every part-time instructor deserves an annual award, if such is handed out, every part-time instructor deserves recognition for those elements of teaching that he or she did well. Such recognition may take the form of a festive e-mail from the department chairperson circulated to everyone in the department, listing the accomplishments of adjuncts; it may be a brief story/report in the school's newsletter; it can also be an informal social gathering at the end of the semester at which individuals are recognized. Whatever the choice of venue, recognizing quality teaching by part-time faculty is a way to help integrate them into the department and a means for reinforcing quality teaching.

Notes

1. Gappa, Judith M., and Leslie, David W. (1993). *The Invisible Faculty*. San Francisco: Jossey-Bass Publishers, pp. 127–128.

2. Foster, David, and Foster, Edith. (1998, Jan–Feb). It's a Buyer's Market: "Disposable Professors," Grade Inflation and Other Problems. *Academe*, 28–25.

TO STUDENTS

Steps in Fostering and Sustaining a Supportive Learning Environment

Action Plans

The Challenge

The quality of teaching and learning has a direct bearing on key institutional issues, and since students are at the center of this matrix, their relationships carry substantial weight when considering the welfare of the school. When students enroll in college they assume, and should have every right to expect, the best-quality education possible. They expect their teachers to be knowledgeable about the subject matter and skilled in teaching it, they view their teachers as representatives of the institution and their most immediate contact persons, and they have no way of distinguishing between a full-time and a part-time instructor. They may not realize that so many of their instructors are the least connected to the school and the least knowledgeable about its culture.

Some key institutional issues, discussed below, can be linked directly to the relationship between teachers and students.

Retention

Students are most likely to drop out of college in the first two years.[1] These are the same two years during which most courses are taught by part-time faculty. In other words, during the time students need to have opportunities to make real and lasting connections to the institution, the most visible links are instructors who themselves are not well connected to the institution. The two options for addressing this dichotomy are either to have only full-time instructors teach freshman- and sophomore-level courses, which may not be feasible for many good reasons, or to enhance part-time faculty's capacity to provide students with the kinds of support they need during this vulnerable period.

Academic Success

With the exception of "late bloomers," most students begin to develop a clear path toward academic success in their freshman year. Study skills, recognition of the differences between college and high school, development of a road map toward a degree, all of these start happening early in college students' lives. These important developments do not happen in a vacuum and certainly not through some automatic or autonomous process. They are embedded in course-taking, college students' fundamental activity, so much of the students' academic success depends on guidance and support from their instructors, in addition to course content. Yet so many of their instructors, having had no pedagogical training and being paid strictly for actual "contact hours," may focus on content delivery, with minimal if any attention to anything else.

Changing Student Demographics

As the makeup of the student body shifts from including predominantly 18- to 22-year-olds fresh out of high school to including and sometimes being dominated by "nontraditional" students—mostly adults in mid-career or women who delayed their education to be stay-at-home-moms—a parallel shift needs to take place in the role of the instructor and the relationship between instructor and students. While attention must still be paid to the need of the traditional student to understand the relevance of academic studies to the world of work, nontraditional students have a very different set of needs. The 18-year-old is looking for ways to ensure a good life; the older student is looking for ways to ensure a better life. Without sufficient training or support, the part-time instructor may naturally gear his or her teaching to one of the two populations rather than seeking a good balance.

Quality Assurance

So much of students' reaction to teachers, teaching, and courses has to do with their sense of being at the center of the teaching/learning situation and of having someone genuinely care about their progress. Those are not always tangible elements, and it is hard to identify them with any specificity in the teaching/learning environment. However, they all seem to revolve around instructors' availability outside of class, the amount of direct communication taking place between teacher and students, and the teachers' ability to "customize" teaching to some degree. Hurried, harried teachers who do not participate in the curriculum development process, who do not have opportunities for formal and informal communication with fellow full-time faculty, and who may not be up on the latest or best teaching resources may not be able to relate to such student needs and expectations. The result is that, knowingly or unwittingly, instructors may set standards that are lower than they should be to assure student satisfaction and, possibly, continued employment.

Overcoming some of these discrepancies between institutional and student expectations and the realities of part-time faculty employment presents some real challenges.

A different type of challenge stems from the unique background of many of the part-time faculty who either are fully employed professionals in their fields or who have worked part of their lives in nonacademic settings. These backgrounds can provide a wealth of opportunities for academic growth of students, yet they are seldom tapped due to the unique and restricted relationship between part-time faculty and academic institutions. The pay-per-teaching-session or -course system defines few contact opportunities with students in two areas that could offer unique advantages when covered by part-time faculty. First, many part-time faculty, by virtue of their firsthand knowledge of the nonacademic world in which students will ultimately function, can be invaluable resources for advising and mentoring. However, their lack of availability can be a barrier. As the Academic Senate for California Community Colleges states in its comprehensive statement about part-time faculty:

> Clearly, if office hours and one-on-one contact with students is so fundamental to the educational process as to place it in the negotiated contracts of full-time faculty members, then the lack of facilities and compensation for such work by part-time faculty members constitutes a deficiency in institutional support of a part-time faculty member's students, thereby creating a *de facto* secondary tier of instructional employees. There is a qualitative differential in the education full-time and part-time faculty members are thereby able to provide to their respective students.[2]

Second, these same external activities by part-time faculty can provide wonderful opportunities for experience-based learning for students, learning that takes place outside the classroom or that brings the outside world into the classroom (face-to-face or virtual). Both of these opportunities are seldom realized because they are not perceived to be part of part-time faculty's "package."

Extensive teaching by part-time faculty, in lower-division courses as well as in specialized advanced courses, presents students with a unique challenge.

In attempting to gain entry into graduate schools or in applying for jobs, they often cannot count on references from some of their most important teachers, simply because they may no longer be accessible. It has also been observed that graduate schools may frown on applications supported mainly by part-time faculty references.

Much has already been covered in this volume about issues related to students, but many were not directly referenced. The following action items may help institutions consider options for addressing these challenges.

Action Plans

Access and Communication

For students to perceive part-time faculty as special as full-time faculty, part-time faculty's invisibility needs to be replaced with clear and continuous presence and accessibility. Some of the ways to achieve this challenging task have been listed earlier and are revisited here to underscore their importance.

Names in Print

Part-time faculty's names should be listed wherever faculty names appear and should always include their institutional e-mail addresses. In addition to the annual catalog, such lists are

- Departmental faculty lists
- Course schedules, in which actual names are used instead of the generic "staff" designation
- Online directories
- Departmental bulletin boards

Teaching Package

As mentioned earlier, part-time faculty's contracts typically call for their presence during face-to-face class sessions or the equivalent in online courses, but rarely during any other occasions in which formal and informal contact between teacher and students takes place. While class sessions may be the obvious and key meeting place, such occasions are not necessarily where most students choose to communicate with their teachers, certainly not about personal learning issues. The teaching "package," then, should include specified times during which part-time faculty are available to their students outside of class and for which they are compensated. Such out-of-class contact time can be in the form of prescribed office hours or accessibility by phone or e-mail; the latter two modes should be accommodated through assigning both an institutional e-mail address and voicemail access. Information regarding out-of-class availability should be clearly communicated to students through the course syllabus and through departmental postings in central locations.

Large-class Support

When full-time faculty teach large classes (more than 50 students), their students have a couple of alternatives for getting more individualized attention: they can visit the instructor's office during posted office hours or as a drop-in, or they have access to information and help through teaching assistants the full-time instructor may employ. These are not usually available in courses taught by part-time faculty.

The challenges of learning in a very large class have been described and discussed. They are further underscored when the course is taught by a part-time instructor who is present only for the duration of each session. One inexpensive solution is the use of volunteer graduate students as discussion leaders and resource persons. In one such project (at Florida International University), graduate students who were not teaching assistants but who nevertheless wanted to gain some teaching experience, volunteered to be small discussion group leaders for a Human Biology class. The enrollment of approximately 340 (mostly) freshmen was broken down into groups of 10–15, each led by a volunteer. The opportunity to participate and ask important questions in that kind of setting had a positive effect on the students; it also provided the instructor with opportunities to communicate with students, via the volunteers, in ways that the large-class format did not allow.

Participation in Major Events

Freshman convocation, where it exists, and graduation ceremonies are two key milestones in the lives of college students; there may be others of a more local nature. Part-time faculty's participation in such events is both appropriate as a means of connecting with the institution and being an integral and public part of it. It is also of great value in communicating to students that part-time faculty are part of the teaching team that views them, the students, as important.

Long-term Contact

Part-time faculty who teach introductory or core courses, or those who teach specialized, preprofessional courses, are often in a good position to provide students with references for a variety of opportunities, including admission to graduate studies, employment, membership in professional organizations, and others. Yet, due to their transitory employment, part-time faculty are not available to provide such references even within a couple of years of having taught, let alone for any longer than that. To provide students with the ability to contact former (part-time) instructors, the department can maintain an archive of part-time faculty contact information. The need for such an archive to be up to date can be explained to part-time faculty, who, for the most part, are flattered to be asked to have a continuing role in their former students' lives.

Advising and Mentoring of Students

Among the many hats faculty wear, the one of informal advisor and mentor is frequently overlooked, especially if these roles are not assigned formally. If feasible, part-time faculty, of course, should be encouraged and expected to provide formal advising as part of their departmental duties. But when this is not possible, informal functions can and should still be expected. For many students, part-time faculty are their only faculty contacts during the freshman year and often during the sophomore year. So such important functions are needed and welcomed, and some are described below.

Advising as Part of Teaching

- Articulating the relationship of the specific course's material to the major or other disciplines
- Ongoing encouragement of students to seek formal advising help from either the central advising office or departmental sources
- Using office hours for informal conversations about students' studies in general—the syllabus could include information about this
- Frequent and ongoing feedback to students about their performance

- Including study tips information in the syllabus—"how to succeed in this course"
- Referring students to sources of information, on the Web or elsewhere, about good study practices in the specific discipline
- Availability of the teacher, by e-mail or in person, to discuss any issues associated with the course, before they affect student performance. Information about this kind of advising should be stated clearly in the syllabus and reiterated throughout the semester.

Mentoring

- Providing a broader view of the importance and the relationship of the particular course to the entire curriculum
- Advice on such matters as time management, priority setting, goal setting
- Information regarding support organizations available to students on campus and possibly through professional organizations
- Teacher's own enthusiasm about the subject matter, the discipline, and lifelong learning

Career Support

- The teacher serves as a role model on two levels—as a teacher and as a professional in the specific discipline.
- Guest teachers are brought in to teach portions of the course or to demonstrate firsthand how the information can be applied in the "real world." Such guest teachers can be selected to represent a broad spectrum of relevant professions.
- As part of their assignments, students may be required to interview professionals in relevant fields.
- Assignments are structured to let students examine information and present results from diverse professional points of view. This is an especially effective strategy for research assignments and group projects.
- Discussion of possible career choices based on the discipline takes place, formally as part of the course, or informally through handouts or referral to information sources.

Another dimension unique to part-time faculty is their ability to connect with their students, due to their involvement in professional activities outside academe, and to provide their students with access to networks. Such networks may serve multiple purposes, from providing settings for course projects to identifying employment opportunities.

Opportunities for Experience-based Learning

Many part-time faculty are simultaneously engaged in teaching and in full-time professional careers outside academe, or they may have been practicing professionals at some point in their lives. Such experience and the professional contacts associated with it can be invaluable in providing students with enhanced educational experiences and in fostering the bond between the part-time teacher and students. As with any activity that goes beyond the typical three-hour course session, part-time faculty need to be encouraged to branch out and bring the world into their courses. Encouragement may be of various types, not just through financial compensation—sometimes it is just a matter of suggesting or asking. As professionals, they are proud of what they do, but their knowledge and experience are too often overlooked and are not tapped.

Some suggestions for expanding experience-based learning opportunities for students appear below.

Service Learning

Unlike many other volunteer activities, this is a way to tie real-life work experience directly to the content of a college course. It provides students with an opportunity to improve academic learning, to apply it in practical situations, and to develop new sets of skills. Part-time faculty possess firsthand knowledge of such ties and connections to community organizations that can be used. The anchor for service learning is the course itself, and the field experiences, while taking place in nonprofit settings, have to be justifiable as an integral part of the curriculum, be pedagogically sound, and be well integrated into the fabric of the course.

Field Trips

Visiting the workplace of an engineer/part-time instructor can add enormous value to a course. Such field trips need to be well planned and preferably preceded by a preview and preparatory work by the students. The experience itself has to be directly related to the course's goals and content and be structured so that students are guided to observe, question, and note specific aspects and details. A follow-up review and assignments should help frame the field experience as a complete learning opportunity.

Internships

When appropriate and applicable to the substance of a course, a short internship experience may add invaluable dimensions and learning opportunities. It is somewhat similar to service learning but, unlike SL, can take place in any professional setting, including corporate or small business.

Field Applications Projects

When a part-time instructor has professional connections in the community, part of the students' assignments can be in the form of projects that bridge theoretical, class content and its applications. Such projects may be research-oriented, using a variety of approaches, including measurements, interviews, surveys, etc.

Problem-based Learning

Problem-based learning (PBL) uses real-life situations as the foundation for learning. Rather than studying a unit of material first (see "Case Studies" below), PBL's approach is to have students grapple with a problem first to determine (1) what they need to learn to address the issues, and (2) how they are going to learn it. This approach encourages students to take responsibility for their own learning.

Problems for PBL are usually developed by the instructor who has in mind specific learning goals. Many part-time faculty, by virtue of their having worked outside academe, are in a good position to develop problems that truly connect theory to practice. The students then bring their own prior knowledge and/or experience into the learning process, integrate them into learning activities, and use resources, including the instructor, to deal with the problem.

Case Studies

Similar to PBL but with a major difference, case studies also help bridge theory and application. Contrary to PBL, however, the problem is presented to students at the conclusion of a unit of study as a way to help them integrate, assess, apply, and evaluate information they have already learned. With this approach, too, part-time faculty can inject a dose of reality based on their own experience.

Notes

1. Swail, Watson Scott. (2004, June 21). *The Art of Student Retention: A Handbook for Practitioners and Administrators.* Texas Higher Education Coordinating Board 20th Annual Recruitment and Retention Conference, Austin, TX, p. 5 (www.educationalpolicy.org).

2. *Part-time Faculty: A Principled Perspective.* (2002, spring). Document adopted by The Academic Senate for California Community Colleges, Sacramento, CA, p. 15 (www.academicsenate.cc.ca.us/Publications/Papers/Downloads/PDFs/Part-Time.pdf).

TO SCHOLARSHIP

Nurturing the Whole Professional—Teacher and Scholar

Action Plans

The Challenge

The primary activity part-time faculty engage in is teaching—that is the reason for their hiring, that is the basis for their pay, and that is the only articulated expectation in many instances. Yet, if part-time faculty are to provide students with the same well-rounded education expected from full-time faculty, and if, as has been suggested, the quality of teaching rises with scholarly activity, then part-time faculty—like their full-time colleagues—should be expected to engage in scholarship. The sad reality is that part-time faculty not only are *not* encouraged to engage in scholarly activities, the current hiring, performance assessment, and remuneration systems are all skewed in favor of discouraging scholarship.

A poll conducted by *Adjunct Advocate Magazine* offers a glimpse into a different reality, one in which part-time faculty actively participate in all forms of scholarship. In this poll, 62 percent of respondents had published scholarly articles, books, or other publications during the preceding year; 60 percent were engaged in research in their respective fields; and 54 percent applied for grants.[1] Obviously, at least part-time faculty themselves are highly interested and motivated to engage in scholarly activities, but this is a well-kept secret.

Another well-kept secret is the awarding of prestigious scholarly grants and fellowships to part-time faculty. Such coveted awards as the Guggenheims and the Fulbrights have gone in recent years to part-time faculty in varied fields. In highlighting recent recipients of the Guggenheims, *Adjunct Advocate Magazine* observed, "winning a Guggenheim is a feather in any faculty member's hat. It is an even more coveted prize for adjunct faculty, who must overcome enormous odds to win [one]."[2]

A true institutional commitment to quality teaching and education requires not only appropriate support systems for part-time faculty as outlined in the previous sections, but also access to and encouragement for ongoing scholarly activity and productivity, much the same as is expected from and celebrated for full-time faculty.

Action Plans

The Scholarship of Teaching

One of the first and most obvious areas in which part-time faculty's contributions can be invaluable is the scholarship of teaching. Briefly, the Scholarship of Teaching and Learning (SoTL) is about applying the same standards and methodologies used in typical academic research activities, but with a focus on investigating issues related to teaching and learning at the college/ university level. As an activity undertaken over time, teaching provides teachers with unique opportunities to investigate it in the same ways that they, as scholars, conduct research in the disciplines.

The Carnegie Foundation for the Advancement of Teaching's SoTL project and the discussion emerging following the publication of Boyer's *Scholarship Reconsidered*[3] have provided the impetus for the introduction and inclusion of SoTL on an increasing number of campuses. As an emerging scholarly field, SoTL still faces numerous challenges, not the least of which is full-time faculty's hesitation to engage in it to the exclusion of "traditional" scholarship. Such hesitation is understandable in light of institutional insistence on traditional scholarly pursuits as the only ones used in evaluating professional accomplishments and, consequently, in making tenure and promotion decisions. Additionally, many full-time faculty tend to separate their teaching and scholarship activities and view them as mutually exclusive when it comes to priorities, time allocations, and personal interests.

Part-time faculty, if encouraged and supported, may provide the much needed link between teaching and SoTL. This is so primarily because their professional activity tends to focus on teaching, and because while they have, unfortunately, very little access to the types of resources needed for more traditional research—especially in such areas as the sciences and engineering—their own desire for scholarly activity may be addressed by SoTL.

One way to initiate SoTL activity among part-time faculty is through an internal grants program that allows them to engage in this scholarly undertaking. The grants can be competitive and based on individual or team proposals, or they can be made available across the disciplines to encourage variety and participation. Such grants, provided for single-semester or multi-semester projects, can be expected to produce not only scholarly publications but, more important, immediate and direct benefits to the institution through the dissemination of newly acquired insights into and suggestions for improved quality of teaching and learning. An example of such a program, called Curiosity Mini-Grants, can be found at the University of Nevada, Las Vegas (see http://tlc.unlv.edu/pdfs/sotl_mini_grants_booklet.pdf).

Encouragement for collaboration between part-time and full-time faculty in the development and implementation of SoTL research projects will strengthen the bonds between part-time faculty and the institution.

Access to Information

Of course, access to information regarding scholarship opportunities should not be limited to part-time faculty, so the suggestions below should not be construed as applying exclusively to them. It is the case, however, that due to scheduling and information dissemination patterns at many schools, full-time faculty are more likely than are part-time faculty to be exposed to important information, resulting in their ability to take fuller advantage of opportunities.

Information about scholarship opportunities comes from a variety of sources. With relatively little effort, such information can be made available to part-time faculty on a regular basis through the means described below.

Institutional Support

Many schools have administrative units whose key function is to access information about grant opportunities. These units often offer training in grant proposal writing and related matters. All of their services should be made available to part-time faculty through a variety of channels.

Some of the grant sources that consider adjuncts as recipients are[4]

- John Simon Guggenheim Memorial Foundation—fellowships in the humanities, the natural sciences, the social sciences, and creative arts (www.gf.org/applic.html)
- Fulbright Scholar Program—fellowships for international exchange teaching and research opportunities (www.cies.org)

- National Endowment for the Humanities—several fellowship programs (www.neh.gov/grants/onebook/fellowship)
- National Humanities Center—fellowships for faculty with earned doctorates and a record of publications (www.nhc.rtu.cn.us:8080)
- Mellon Post-doctoral Fellowships—offered through the Penn Humanities Forum at the University of Pennsylvania (humanities.sas.upenn.edu/mellonform.htm)
- Woodrow Wilson International Center for Scholars—research fellowships in areas related to governance (fellowships@wwic.si.edu)
- American Association for the Advancement of Science—fellowships in science and technology policy (fellowships.aaas.org/application.html)
- National Science Foundation (Societal Dimensions in Engineering, Science and Technology Program)—research fellowships focused on ethics, values, or the uses of science and engineering (www.fastlane.nsf.gov/dllMenu.htm)
- Library of Congress—fellowships for research using its foreign-languages collection (www.acls.org/appform.htm)
- National Endowment for the Arts—fellowships for creative writers and translators (arts.endow.gov/guidefLit03/PDFFirst.html)

Web Sources

Grant and fellowship resources are posted more often on a variety of sites on the World Wide Web. The scope of data includes

- Information about grant sources
- Opportunities for publication
- Professional associations, including those whose primary focus is pedagogy in particular disciplines
- Professional conferences and seminars—when adjuncts' scholarly activities qualify them for participation in professional conferences, effort should be made to make financial support (stipends) available to them that will allow for such participation; their involvement will enhance the reputation of the department and the institution

Bringing such information to the attention of part-time faculty may in itself suggest the desirability of their engagement in scholarly activities.

Scholarly Publications

For those part-time faculty who have never engaged in scholarly activity or who have not gone through the process of obtaining a doctoral degree (which provides certain grounding in research and scholarly writing), it is important to become familiar with key publications in their field. This, in turn, helps them stay current in their fields and develop ideas for possible scholarly activities of their own. Some institutions have active networks of departmental library liaisons whose function is to advise the library of publications it should acquire for the specific disciplines; they also function as conduits of information from the library to the departments about changes in the information environment. Too often, all of this important information is not available to part-time faculty. Including them in the departmental discussions of journals, books, and other scholarly resources to be acquired can create important bonds.

Field Applications

A unique aspect of part-time faculty's professional lives is often overlooked as a potential source for scholarship. Since so many part-time faculty are full-time professionals in the nonacademic world, or may have retired from this arena, they have access to both research opportunities and funding sources for such research. Collaborative academic/business research and scholarship opportunities "brokered" by part-time faculty, and in which they are active participants, have not been truly explored for their potential. Such opportunities should, of course, involve full-time faculty as partners whenever appropriate. With some creative thinking and entrepreneurial initiative, such collaborations may prove to be a new and productive source of scholarship for many departments.

Professional Portfolios

An earlier discussion addressed the benefits of teaching portfolios. An expanded application of the same concept can integrate scholarly activity into the picture while simultaneously encouraging such activity. A professional portfolio could include, in addition to aspects of teaching, other components such as

- Examples of the relationship between the part-time instructor's teaching and professional activities
- Examples of curriculum enhancements based on professional and scholarly activities
- Discussion of professional service activities
- Scholarly publications
- Reports about scholarly activities such as attendance at conferences or professional seminars

Advanced Degree Completion

A valued colleague should always be encouraged to engage in activities that lead to continuous professional growth. For part-time faculty who for one reason or another have not completed a terminal degree, be it a doctorate or a master's, engaging in further study does promote scholarly engagement. Whenever possible, part-time faculty should be encouraged to continue and complete their graduate studies; as a matter of fact, every effort should be made to create opportunities for support in this area. Some ideas for support include:

- Tuition remission or waiver for full- or part-time graduate studies
- Academic advising to encourage uninterrupted progress
- Accommodation in scheduling to assist in juggling teaching and studying responsibilities
- Mentoring support if the area of study is linked to the department in which the part-time instructor is teaching

Shared Knowledge

Scholarship can be a lonely pursuit or a collegial undertaking. While much research and writing is done in isolation, one purpose of all scholarship is dissemination. Public acknowledgment of scholarly activity by part-time faculty can serve as a catalyst for further activity. Opportunities for sharing scholarly activities and information about them are not hard to find. They may include

- Inviting part-time faculty to join scholarly activities directed by full-time faculty

- Inviting part-time faculty, especially those engaged in professional activities outside academe, to review and comment on scholarly activities by full-time faculty and by graduate students
- Inviting part-time faculty to share results of their scholarly activities with the whole department
- Inviting part-time faculty to share results of their scholarly activities with faculty across the institution during faculty forums and similar opportunities
- Publicly acknowledging part-time faculty's scholarly activities and achievements through institutional information channels
- Informing colleagues in the department of part-time faculty's professional accomplishments (promotions, participation in conferences, etc.) in their nonacademic lives

Notes

1. *Adjunct Advocate Magazine* (http://adjunctnation.com/archive/poll/vote/past).

2. Boyer, E. L. (1990). *Scholarship Reconsidered: Priorities of the Professoriate.* Princeton, NJ: Carnegie Foundation for the Advancement of Teaching.

3. Cumo, Chris. (2002, July/August). Yes, Virginia, Adjuncts Do Win Guggenheims. *Adjunct Advocate Magazine,* 12.

4. Cumo, Chris. (2001, September/October). 10 National Fellowships Open to Temporary Faculty. *Adjunct Advocate Magazine,* 18–20.

EPILOGUE

Parting Thoughts

It is unlikely that issues related to part-time faculty will diminish or disappear in the foreseeable future. Three distinct reasons can account for this certainty. First, once established and operated for a length of time, a practice such as the use of part-time faculty is hard to give up. "Don't fix that which does not need fixing" is a common mantra in institutional life—things are running relatively smoothly, so let's not even think about any meaningful changes.

A second reason for maintaining the status quo is based on simple economic realities. Short-term responses and solutions and expedient approaches are the easiest ways to address budgetary constraints and economic cycles. Yes, quality is important, and so is adherence to academic standards and good practice, but let's wait until the current financial crisis is over before we consider change.

A third reason for continuing long-standing practices is the evolution of higher education as a right and as an expectation. In the first half of the 20th century, a high school diploma was seen as the key to a lifetime of employment for a sizable majority of young people. If you had a high school diploma, you were considered "trainable" in many industries and for many professions. With the introduction and phenomenal growth of community colleges, starting in the 1960s, much vocational training that used to take place in high schools was taken over by the two-year schools. Soon after, an associate of arts (AA) degree became the "passport" to a life of steady employment. It was not long, however, before community colleges, while still seen as producing professionals in many trades, were transformed into something quite different. A blurring of the lines between community colleges and junior colleges occurred—as a matter of fact, many junior colleges, whose primary goal was to prepare students for the four-year "senior" college, were converted into community colleges. As societal expectations rose for the four-year college degree to become the stamp of an educated person, and thereby to practically guarantee employability, enrollment pressures on both two-year and four-year institutions created an ever-growing need for part-time faculty. There are some signs that public perceptions may be moving still further "upward" in that a graduate degree may be the true "door opener" for well-paid employment. Recent statistics on the relative income levels of professionals with varying educational levels are but one measure of such perceptions.

So the use of part-time faculty is here to stay for the foreseeable future, and the onus is on administrators and faculty developers to identify and find ways to ensure that short-term expediency does not come at the expense of long-term quality. This volume has suggested a variety of strategies and practices to address the complex issues inherent in using part-time faculty. Some strategies, no doubt, will require additional financial resources; many others will only require the will and creativity to implement meaningful changes. In the end, decisions will have to be made based on specific criteria and will have to answer fundamental questions:

- What is best for our students?
- What is quality education, and how can it be achieved?
- What is equitable for our faculty?
- What type of academic culture does our institution want to foster?
- How can we integrate the advantages inherent in using part-time faculty while minimizing the drawbacks?

BIBLIOGRAPHY

The following bibliography contains three major groups of resources:

- *Books and monographs.* Included are most of the publications available on the subject of adjunct faculty. The vast majority of these focus on the realities of adjunct life and practice, reflecting the scarcity of resources dedicated to change and improvement in this area.
- *Selected unpublished doctoral dissertations.* This section provides a rich resource of studies encompassing, in addition to the realities of adjunct faculty, examination of performance and suggested improvements. The dissertations included here are mostly from the 1990s on; however, many earlier ones can be accessed as well.
- *Selected articles and reports.* Spanning approximately the last 12 years, resources in this section include key national reports and a variety of representative essays and news reports.

Books and Monographs

Baldwin, Roger G., and Jay L. Chronister. *Teaching Without Tenure—Policies and Practices for a New Era.* Baltimore, MD: Johns Hopkins University Press, 2001.

Benjamin, Ernst, ed., *Exploring the Role of Contingent Instructional Staff in Undergraduate Learning.* New Directions for Higher Education No. 123. San Francisco: Jossey-Bass Publishers, 2003.

Bianco-Mathis, Virginia, and Neal Chalofsky, eds., *The Adjunct Faculty Handbook.* Thousand Oaks, CA: Sage Publications, 1996.

Biles, George E., and Howard P. Tuckman. *Part-Time Faculty Personnel Management Policies.* New York: American Council on Education/Macmillan Publishing Company, 1986.

Boyer, E. L. *Scholarship Reconsidered: Priorities of the Professoriate.* Princeton, NJ: Carnegie Foundation for the Advancement of Teaching, 1990.

Carroll, Jill. *How to Survive as an Adjunct Lecturer.* Houston, TX: Adjunct Solutions, 2001.

Dubson, Michael, ed., *Ghosts in the Classroom—Stories of College Adjunct Faculty and the Price We All Pay*. Boston: Camel's Back Books, 2001.

Gappa, Judith M. *Part-Time Faculty: Higher Education at a Crossroads*. Washington, DC: Association for the Study of Higher Education Report #3, 1984.

Gappa, Judith M., and David W. Leslie. *The Invisible Faculty—Improving the Status of Part-Timers in Higher Education*. San Francisco: Jossey-Bass Publishers, 1993.

Grieve, Donald E. *A Handbook for Adjunct/Part-Time Faculty and Teachers of Adults*. Elyria, OH: Info-Tec, 2001.

Greive, Donald E., and Catherine A. Worden, eds., *Managing Adjunct & Part-Time Faculty for the New Millennium*. Elyria, OH: Info-Tec, 2000.

Leslie, David W. *The Growing Use of Part-Time Faculty: Understanding Causes and Effects*. San Francisco: Jossey-Bass Publishers, 1998.

Leslie, David W., Samuel E. Kellams, and G. Manny Gunne. *Part-Time Faculty in American Higher Education*. New York: Praeger Publishers, 1982.

Lyons, Richard E., Marcella L. Kysilka, and George E. Pawlas. *The Adjunct Professor's Guide to Success*. Boston: Allyn and Bacon, 1999.

Nelson, Cary, ed. *Will Teach for Food—Academic Labor in Crisis*. Minneapolis, MN: University of Minnesota Press, 1997.

Schell, Eileen E., and Patricia Lambert Stock, eds., *Moving a Mountain: Transforming the Role of Contingent Faculty in Composition Studies and Higher Education*. Urbana, IL: National Council of Teachers of English, 2001.

Swail, Watson Scott. *The Art of Student Retention: A Handbook for Practitioners and Administrators*. Austin, TX: Texas Higher Education Coordinating Board 20th Annual Recruitment and Retention Conference, June 21, 2004. (www.educationalpolicy.org)

Tinto, Vincent. *Leaving College: Rethinking the Causes and Cures of Student Attrition*. Chicago: University of Chicago Press, 1993.

Wallin, Desna L., ed., *Adjunct Faculty in Community Colleges*. Bolton, MA: Anker, 2005.

Wilke, Arthur S. *The Hidden Professoriate*. Westport, CT: Greenwood Press, 1979.

Wilke, Arthur S. *Part-time Faculty: A Principled Perspective*. Document adopted by The Academic Senate for California Community Colleges, CA: Spring 2002, www.academicsenate.cc.ca.us/Publications/Papers/Downloads/PDFs/Part-Time .pdf.

Selected Unpublished Doctoral Dissertations

Adams, Deborah Ann. "The Relationship Between Use of Varying Proportions of Part-Time Faculty and Full-Time Nursing Faculty Perceptions of Workload and Collegial Support." PhD diss., University of Maryland, 1992.

Ashford, Gayla Brown. "Perceptions of Administrators, Full-Time Faculty, and Part-Time Faculty Regarding the Economic Implications of the Future of Part-Time Faculty in Alabama's State Community Colleges." EdD diss., University of Alabama, 1993.

Augusta, Virginia Leigh. "The Growing Stratification of the Academic Labor Market: Is There Permeability from the Non-Tenure-Track to the Tenure-Track Ranks?" PhD diss., Cornell University, 2005.

Avery, Fay Ross. "A Study of the Criteria Used in Evaluating Adjunct Faculty Within the Virginia Community College System." EdD diss., George Washington University, 1991.

Barden, Lillian. "Part-Time Faculty in Business: Profiles, Perceptions, and Potential. A Study of Part-time Instructors in Business Degree Programs in the San Francisco Bay Area." PhD diss., Golden Gate University, 1988.

Backford-Yanes, Carolyn A. "How Adjunct Faculty's Professional Work Experience Affects the Community College Learning Environment." PhD diss., Colorado State University, 2005.

Berning, Phyllis Margaret. "A Study of Intellectual Capital: Adjunct Faculty in Minnesota Colleges." EdD diss., University of Minnesota, 2001.

Berry, Joe Tracy. "Contingent Faculty in Higher Education: An Organizing Strategy and Chicago Area Proposal." PhD diss., Union Institute and University, 2002.

Bogert, Dorothea Taylor. "Use of Part-Time/Adjunct Faculty in Community Colleges: A Multi-Case Study of Three Florida Community Colleges." PhD diss., Florida State University, 2004.

Bohm, Berndt Harry. "The Effects of Student Ratings in Modifying Part-Time Faculty Instruction." EdD diss., University of Virginia, 1984.

Bonesteel, Margaret Davidson. "Part-Time Travellers: The Impact of Organizational Culture on Part-Time Faculty Socialization and Satisfaction." EdD diss., Syracuse University, 1994.

Bowman, Linda Speier. "Work Satisfaction and Group Differences: Full-Time and Part-Time Faculty in Community Colleges." PhD diss., University of Colorado at Denver, 1995.

Buffaloe, Laura Walton. "An Analysis of the North Carolina Community College System Policies and Practices for Part-Time Faculty." EdD diss., Virginia Polytechnic Institute and State University, 1995.

Burbano, Cheryl Marie. "The Effects of Different Forms of Student Ratings Feedback on Subsequent Student Ratings of Part-Time Faculty." PhD diss., University of Florida, 1987.

Burke, William Arthur. "Comparative Job Satisfaction of Full-Time and Part-Time Faculty at Three Selected Rhode Island Colleges." EdD diss., University of Sarasota, 1989.

Cain, Michael Scott. "Integrating Adjunct Faculty into a Community College Humanities Division: An Organization Development Model." PhD diss., University of Maryland, 1991.

Carroll, Susan Caye. "Perceived Importance of Non-Monetary Incentives to Part-Time Faculty Motivation in Community Colleges." PhD diss., University of Texas at Austin, 1985.

Casablanca-Torres, Mercedes. "The Relationship of Education and Experience to Teaching Effectiveness of Part-Time and Full-Time Faculty Members as Perceived by Students." PhD diss., New York University, 1987.

Charumanee, Nicom. "The Perceived Professional Development Needs of Nebraska Public Two-Year College Full-Time and Part-Time Vocational Instructors." PhD diss., University of Nebraska, 1986.

Coffey, Susan Osborn. "Part-Time Faculty Policies and Procedures in Public Community Colleges in Virginia." EdD diss., University of Virginia, 1992.

Cooper, Rene Victor. "An Economic Analysis of Part-Time Faculty Employment in Florida's Public Community Colleges." PhD diss., Florida State University, 1986.

Cowen, Elaine Walda. "Perceptions of Part-Time Nursing Faculty and Administrators Related to Job Satisfaction." EdD diss., Ball State University, 1991.

Davis, Barbara S. "Proactive Administrative Strategies for Adjunct Faculty Equality." PhD diss., Capella University, 2005.

Denman, Sarah N. "Role Prescriptions of Part-Time Faculty in Community Colleges: A Comparison of Interpretations of Role Prescriptions of Part-Time Faculty Held by Part-time Faculty and Department Chairpersons in Community Colleges." EdD diss., West Virginia University, 1986.

Fabisinski, Nancy Masdon. "The Role of Part-Time Faculty in Alabama Community College English Departments: Perceptions of Administrators and Part-time Teachers." EdD diss., University of Alabama, 1994.

Faulkner, Susan Lynch. "An Analysis of the Inservice Education Needs to Develop Instructional Skills of Part-Time Business Faculty." EdD diss., Virginia Polytechnic Institute and State University, 1990.

Fisher, Deena K. "The Proper Care and Feeding of Adjunct Faculty. A Qualitative Multi-Site Case Study: The Integration of Part-Time Adjunct Faculty within the Hierarchical Organization of Higher Education." EdD diss., Oklahoma State University, 2005.

Forrest, Thomas Ward. "Part-Time Music Faculty in Selected Senior Institutions of Higher Education in the Commonwealth of Virginia." EdD diss., College of William and Mary, 1994.

Franklin, Joseph W. "The Attributes, Teaching Effectiveness, and Educational

Commitment of Part-Time Faculty in North Carolina Community Colleges." EdD diss., East Tennessee State University, 1994.

Fulton, Richard Charles. "A Case Study of Adjunct Faculty Members Who Participated in a Semester-Long Staff Development Program at a Community College." EdD diss., University of Maryland College Park, 1999.

Garcia, Steven N. "Academic Program Staffing and Part-Time Faculty in Four-Year Institutions." EdD diss., University of Washington, 1993.

Garcy, Anthony M., Jr. "Part-Time and Contingent Academic Employment." PhD diss., University of Illinois at Chicago, 2002.

Goldbert, Eunice Diane. "Selection and Support of Part-Time Faculty in Illinois Community Colleges: A Study of the Processes That Promote Quality Instruction." PhD diss., Northwestern University, 1990.

Gordon, Carolyn Elizabeth. "Professional Development Need Beliefs of Part-Time Teachers of English." PhD diss., Kent State University, 1990.

Hajduk, Marcia A. "Differences Between Full and Part-Time Faculties' Student-Centered Instructional Format as Identified by PALS and APALS When Teaching Adults in Academic Credit Courses in a Community College." EdD diss., Temple University, 2000.

Hall, Dennis Gerald. "Community College Students' Perceptions of the Teaching Ability of Part-Time Faculty." PhD diss., Colorado State University, 1995.

Hamilton, Stephen Secord. "Part-Time Credit Faculty in Oregon Community Colleges: A Study of Their Utilization and Treatment." PhD diss., University of Oregon, 1994.

Haper, Carole Morgan. "The Part-Time Experience: Professional Women in a Community College." PhD diss., Ohio State University, 2000.

Haring, George Edward. "A Study of Clinical Supervision and the Instructional Effectiveness of Part-Time Community College Faculty." PhD, diss., University of Iowa, 1990.

Herbst, Mary Ann. "The Career Perspective of Dependent Part-Time Faculty." PhD diss., Michigan State University, 1994.

Herron, Gladies Lee. "Adjunct Faculty: Identification of Significant Policy Issues for Tennessee's Public 2-Year Institutions." EdD diss., Peabody College for Teachers at Vanderbilt University, 1992.

Hiemstra, Kathleen Marie. "Use of Part-Time Faculty in Accounting and Business Administration Baccalaureate Programs." PhD diss., University of Pittsburgh, 1985.

Holguin-Balogh, Diana. "Investment Theory Model Application to Assess Adjunct Faculty Job Satisfaction, Commitment, and Turnover." PhD diss., Colorado State University, 1993.

Hoss, Cynthia Joan. "The Mentoring and Professional Development of Part-Time Faculty." EdD diss., University of Nebraska–Lincoln, 1998.

Inglis, David L. "Job Satisfaction Among California Community College Part-Time Faculty Relative to Reasons for Teaching and Types of Courses Taught." EdD diss., University of La Verne, 1992.

Jackson, James Willard. "The Relationship Between Part-Time Faculty and Full-Time Faculty Ratios and Selected Variables in Illinois Community Colleges." PhD diss., Southern Illinois University at Carbondale, 1988.

Jackson, Levi Julius, III. "A Study of the Effectiveness of Occupational-Technical Full-Time and Part-Time Faculty." PhD diss., University of Texas at Austin, 1999.

Jackson, Nancy Vazac. "A Survey of Part-Time Faculty in Baccalaureate Schools of Nursing and Their Learning Needs." EdD diss., Columbia University Teachers College, 1996.

Johnson, Cynthia Smyth. "A Comparison of the Teaching Styles of Full-Time and Part-Time Community College Faculty." EdD diss., Florida Atlantic University, 1999.

Johnson, Mellania. "A Perceptual Study of Part-time Faculty in Alabama's State Community Colleges: Toward Improving Instructional Quality." EdD diss., University of Alabama, 1996.

Kappes, Marilyn Madison. "A Comparison of Students' Ratings of Full- and Part-Time Instructors' Teaching Effectiveness in a Community College." PhD diss., University of Pittsburgh, 1988.

Keister, Lekha George. "Perceptions of Academic Administrators Regarding Part-Time Faculty Employment in Selected Undergraduate Programs of Business and English." PhD diss., State University of New York at Buffalo, 1985.

Kemp, Thomas. "Student Interaction with Part-Time and Full-Time Faculty in Introductory Economics Courses." PhD diss., University of North Texas, 1994.

Kirker, Martha Jane. "Variance in Student Ratings of Part-Time and Full-Time Instructor Effectiveness by Teaching Field and Function at a Midwestern Community College." PhD diss., Iowa State University, 1990.

Klenk, Michelle Grose. "The Development Needs of Part-Time Faculty as Perceived by Part-Time Faculty and Higher Education Administrators." EdD diss., West Virginia University, 1995.

Kuchera, Michael Edward. "An Analysis of Multiple Work Roles and Identities of Adjunct Faculty in American Two-year Colleges." PhD diss., Loyola University of Chicago, 1987.

Law, Frederick Wing-Kai. "A Comparative Analysis of Teaching Effectiveness Between Part-Time and Full-Time Faculty in Selected Ohio Two-Year Colleges." PhD diss., Ohio University, 1987.

Lesniak, Stephen L. "Active Learning and Other Teaching Activities as Perceived by

Part-Time Faculty and Students in a Professional Degree Program Designed for Adult Learners." EdD diss., University of La Verne, 1995.

Levy, Murray. "The Socialization and Integration of the Part-Time Faculty into Department and Campus Life at Glendale Community College." PhD diss., University of Southern California, 1993.

Lewis, Elizabeth Ussery. "Institutional Support Values and Needs as Identified by Adjunct Faculty in a Suburban Texas Community College District." EdD diss., Sam Houston State University, 2000.

Liftin, Harvey F. "The Development and Implementation of an In-Service Model to Assist Part-Time Faculty in Teaching Science Laboratory Courses." EdD diss., Florida International University, 1992.

Loh, Katherine. "Socialization Experiences of Part-Time Faculty: A Study of Socialization Programs and Employment Longevity." PhD diss., American University, 2004.

Longstreth, Susan. "Predicting the Teaching Success of New Part-Time Community College Faculty." PhD diss., Colorado State University, 1992.

Macaulay, Barbara A. Eddy. "Perceptions of Effective Adult Learning: A Case Study Emphasizing the Views of Part-Time Faculty." EdD diss., Columbia University Teachers College, 1995.

Merkle, Rodney Dean. "The Community College Adjunct Faculty Member at the Rural, Off-campus Site: An Overview." PhD diss., Kansas State University, 2001.

Miller, Derehtha Sharon. "The Impact of the Preponderance of Part-Time Faculty on the Mission of the Community College." PhD diss., University of Arizona, 1992.

Miller, Robert James. "The Effects of Part-Time Faculty on Student Involvement and Student Estimate of Gains." EdD diss., Temple University, 1989.

Milliron, Mark David. "Toward a Model of Part-time Faculty Integration in American Community Colleges." PhD diss., University of Texas at Austin, 1995.

Mojock, Charles Raymond. "An Investigation of the Characteristics of Part-Time Faculty in Florida Community Colleges." EdD diss., University of Central Florida, 1990.

Morrison, Elizabeth. "Integration of Adjunct Faculty into the Culture of a Metropolitan Community College: An Analysis." EdD diss., University of Central Florida, 2000.

Murphy, James Kenneth. "Comparison of Policies and Procedures for Selection and Hiring of Full-Time and Part-Time Faculty." PhD diss., University of Missouri–Kansas City, 1992.

Naquin, Deborah Ann. "Educational Technology Integration: Administrator, Full-Time Faculty, and Part-Time Faculty Perspectives as Viewed Through Gender and Position Type." EdD diss., George Washington University, 2001.

Nolte, Jeffrey Lance. "Effects of Inservice Training on Part-Time Continuing Education Faculty." PhD diss., Kansas State University, 1994.

Oblinski, Linda Jean. "Professional Staff Development of Part-Time Faculty at Four Year Colleges and Universities." PhD diss., Marquette University, 1998.

Olson, Andrea Mary. "The Influence of Job Satisfaction on Part-Time Faculty's Commitment to the Collegiate Function of Community Colleges." PhD diss., University of Minnesota, 1996.

Painchaud, Steven Richard. "Part-Time Faculty Teaching in Graduate Management Programs in New England." EdD diss., Boston College, 1993.

Patchke, Timothy O. "A Study of Current Policies and Practices Relating to the Employment of Part-Time Faculty in the Nation's Community Colleges." EdD diss., Rutgers The State University of New Jersey–New Brunswick, 1989.

Pink, Joseph Emmett. "Inservice Needs of Part-Time Vocational Trade and Industry Instructors as Perceived by Vocational Administrators and Part-Time Instructors in the State of Missouri." PhD diss., University of Missouri–Columbia, 1989.

Pluchinotta, Joseph S. "Considerations on Policy Formulation Regarding the Utilization of Part-Time/Adjunct Faculty Within Private, Independent Institutions of Higher Education." PhD diss., University of New Mexico, 1986.

Reddick, Haul M. "Motivation of Part-Time Faculty to Teach in a Community College Setting." EdD diss., Northern Arizona University, 1989.

Reed, Karen Ann. "Perceptions of Professional Development and Institutional Integration by Part-Time Faculty and College Administrators at a Multi-Campus Community College." PhD diss., University of Akron, 1990.

Reid, Steven Sallace. "The Staffing and Enculturation of Adjunct Faculty in Higher Education." EdD diss., Texas A&M University–Commerce, 1996.

Resch, Sharon Lingle. "Status of Full- and Part-Time Business Faculty at Two-Year Colleges and Perceived Importance of Selected Professional Services." PhD diss., Southern Illinois University at Carbondale, 2000.

Rose, Steven Michael. "The Use of Adjunct Faculty in the Community College: A Grounded Theory Analysis." EdD diss., Rutgers The State University of New Jersey–New Brunswick, 1992.

Schell, Eileen Elizabeth. "Gypsy Academics and Motherteachers: Part-Time Women Teachers in Composition Studies." PhD diss., University of Wisconsin–Milwaukee, 1993.

Schwartze, Carolyn Cottrell. "A Comparison of Teaching Goals of Full-Time and Part-Time College Faculty." PhD diss., Saint Louis University, 1996.

Shaffer, Kathryn Louise. "Savior or Servant—What Is the Role of Part-Time Faculty?" PhD diss., Michigan State University, 1995.

Sheppard, Pamela Ann. "The Use of Part-Time Faculty in Associate Degree Nursing, Social Science, and Biological Science Programs." PhD diss., University of North Texas, 1990.

Shriver, Kay Arleen. "A Study of Pre-Employment Assessment Process Used to Select Part-time Faculty for an Allied Health Degree Completion Program." EdD diss., Northern Illinois University, 1993.

Smotroff, Larry Joel. "Part-Time Faculty Development: The Impact of Different Instructional Strategies on Intention, Attitudes, and Beliefs." PhD diss., University of Connecticut, 1996.

Snyder, Barbara Dourte. "The Development of Policies Relative to the Use of Part-Time Faculty at Wilmington College." EdD diss., University of Delaware, 1989.

Soehnlen, Joyce Kathleen. "Phenomenological Investigation of Role Perceptions of the Part-Time Clinical Nurse Educator." PhD diss., University of Akron, 1994.

Spinetta, Katrin Ingeborg. "The Professionalization of Part-Time Faculty in the California Community Colleges." EdD diss., University of California, Berkeley, 1988.

Stokley, Sue Edmonds. "The Frequency of Part-Time Faculty Utilization and the Types of Support Services Provided Them in Two-Year Technical Colleges in South Carolina." EdD diss., University of South Carolina, 1990.

Stringer, Bobbi Rhe. "Nonverbal Immediacy as a Predictor of Student Retention Rates Among Full-Time/Part-Time Community College Faculty." EdD diss., University of North Texas, 1997.

Taylor-King, Sheila. "Differences Between Full- and Part-Time Faculty in the Practice of and Value for Learner-Centered Teaching: A Case Study at a Private Urban Liberal Arts College." EdD diss., University of Wyoming, 2001.

Thomas, Stephen Darrell. "A Professional Development Model for Part-Time Faculty in Community Colleges." PhD diss., University of Texas at Austin, 1986.

Thornton, Catherine. "Issues of Dissonance and Congruence Relating to Institutional Goals Between Part-Time Faculty, Full-Time Faculty and Administrators at a Suburban Institution of Higher Education." EdD diss., Columbia University Teachers College, 1996.

Trent, Bill L. "Community College Students' Evaluations of the Teaching Skills of Part-Time Versus Full-Time Instructors." PhD diss., Kansas State University, 1984.

Valent, Rosemarie Morochko. "Community College Part-Time Faculty: Factors Which Influence Their Expressed Staff Development Needs." EdD diss., Widener University, 1992.

Vitale, Concetta T. "Faculty Development and Support Services Needs of Community College Part-Time Faculty." PhD diss., University of Pittsburgh, 1995.

Wagner, Patricia Anne. "Adjunct Faculty, Innovation, and the Writing Curriculum in Two Rural Community Colleges." PhD diss., Cornell University, 1994.

Weaver, Susan J. Marnell. "The Relationship Between Administrators' Perceptions of Part-Time Faculty and Utilization of Part-Time Faculty at West Virginia Public and Private Colleges and Universities." EdD diss., West Virginia University, 2000.

Wilbanks, Jacqueline Elaine Dion. "Job Satisfaction Among Part-Time Faculty at Selected Four-Year Institutions in Ohio." PhD diss., University of Akron, 1994.

Willenbrock, Paul Karl. "The Impact of Collective Bargaining on Part-Time Higher Education Faculty." EdD diss., University of Massachusetts, 1991.

Williams, James P. "Community College Part-Time Faculty Self-Perceptions of Teaching Performance." EdD diss., Northern Arizona University, 1991.

Williams, Marcia Dean Watford. "Student Perceptions of Effective Instructional Behaviors Displayed by Community College Part-Time Faculty Members and the Part-Time Faculty Members' Participation in Professional Development Activities." EdD diss., University of Southern Mississippi, 1995.

Williams, Michael Mearing. "A Study of Part-Time Faculty at a Large Urban Institution." EdD diss., University of Akron, 1996.

Woodberry, Peter Norman. "From Novice to Expert: Intentional Changes of Part-Time Instructors in a Community College Setting." PhD diss., University of Connecticut, 1991.

Yuen, JoAnn Wai Lung. "Teachers of the Night: Part-Time Faculty in Hawaii Community Colleges." EdD diss., University of Southern California, 2000.

Zink, Glenda J. "A Look at Job Satisfaction Among Part-Time Faculty in Ohio's Two-Year Technical and Community Colleges: The Neglected Majority." EdD diss., University of Akron, 1991.

Zoghi, Cindy. "Labor Markets in Higher Education." PhD diss., University of Texas, 2000.

Selected Articles and Reports

Adjunct Advocate Magazine Poll. (1994). http://adjunctnation.com/archive/poll/?vid=7&vote_result=true.

Altbach, P. G. "The Pros and Cons of Hiring 'Taxicab' Professors." *Chronicle of Higher Education*, January 6, 1995, sec. B, p. 3.

American Association of University Professors. "The Status of Part-Time Faculty." Washington, DC: Author (1980).

American Association of University Professors. (1993). "The Status of Non-Tenure-Track Faculty." A report of the Association's Committee on Part-Time and Non-Tenure-Track Appointments, p. 44. http://www.aaup.org/statements/Redbook/Rbnonten.htm.

American Association of University Professors. "Guidelines for Good Practice: Part-Time and Non-Tenure-Track Faculty." Washington, DC: Author (2003).

American Association of University Professors. "Statement from the Conference on the Growing Use of Part-Time and Adjunct Faculty." *AAUP Bulletin* 84, no. 1 (Jan./Feb. 1998).

American Association of University Professors Committee on Government Relations. "State Legislation Affecting Part-Time Faculty." Washington, DC: AAUP (2001).

American Association of University Professors. AAUP Proposes New Institutional Regulation on Part-Time Appointments, September 2006 (http://www.aaup .org/AAUP/newsroom/pressreleases/PRContingentRIR.htm).

American Federation of Teachers. "The Vanishing Professor." Higher Education Department Report (1998). Washington, DC: Author.

American Historical Association. (1999). "Who Is Teaching in U.S. College Classrooms?" A Collaborative Study of Undergraduate Faculty. http://www.theaha .org/caw/pressrelease.htm.

Arden, E. "Ending the Loneliness and Isolation of Adjunct Professors." *Chronicle of Higher Education*, July 21, 1995, sec. A, p. 44.

Avakian, A. Nancy. "Conflicting Demands for Adjunct Faculty." *Community College Journal* 65, no. 6 (1995):34–36.

Bach, Pamela. "Part-Time Faculty Are Here to Stay." *Planning for Higher Education* 27, no. 3 (1999):32–41.

Berver, K., D. Kurtz, and E. Orton. "Off the Track, But in the Fold." *Academe* 78, no. 6 (1992):27–29.

Bonham, G. "Part-Time Faculty: A Mixed Blessing." *Change* 14, no. 3 (1982):10–11.

Burgess, L. A., and C. Samuels. "Impact of Full-Time Versus Part-Time Instructor Status on College Student Retention and Academic Performance in Sequential Courses." *Community College Journal of Research & Practice* 23 (1999):5.

Burnstad, Helen, and Joseph L. Gadberry. "Retention of Part-Time Faculty." In *Adjunct Faculty in Community Colleges*, Desna L. Wallin, 113–126. Bolton, MA: Anker (2005).

Byrne, Peter J. "Academic Freedom of Part-Time Faculty." *Journal of College and University Law* 27, no. 3 (2001):583–593.

Cain, M. S. "Toward a Theory and a Model for Integrating Part-Time Faculty into a Community College Humanities Division." *Community College Review* 16, no. 3 (1988):42–47.

Carroll, Jill. 2001. "As an Adjunct, Your Eggs Should Be in More Than One Basket." *Chronicle of Higher Education.* http://chronicle.com/jobs/2001/12/2001 121001c.htm.

Cayton, M. K. "Writing as Outsiders: Academic Discourse and Marginalized Faculty." *College English* 53, no. 6 (1991):647–660.

Charfauros, Kenneth H., and William G. Tierney. "Part-Time Faculty in Colleges and Universities: Trends and Challenges in a Turbulent Environment." *Journal of Personnel Evaluation in Education* 13, no. 2 (1999):141–151.

Cohen, Marlene C. "Benefits on a Budget: Addressing Adjunct Needs." Paper presented at the Annual Meeting of the Speech Communication Association, Chicago, IL, Oct. 29–Nov. 1, 1992.

Cumo, Chris. "10 National Fellowships Open to Temporary Faculty." *Adjunct Advocate* (Sept./Oct. 2001):18–20.

Cumo, Chris. "Yes, Virginia, Adjuncts Do Win Guggenheim Awards." *Adjunct Advocate* (July/August 2002):12.

DeBard, R. "Motivating Part-Time Faculty Performance." *OATYC Journal* 15 (1990): 21–23.

DeSevo, M. "Part-Time Nursing Faculty: Suggestions for Change." *Journal of Nursing Education* 34, no. 7 (1995):294–296.

Drago, Robert, and Joan Williams. "A Half-Time Tenure Track Proposal." *Change* 32, no. 6 (2000):46–51.

Elman, Sandra E. "Part-Time Faculty and Student Learning: A Regional Accreditation Perspective." *Peer Review* 5, no. 1, (Fall 2002):15–17.

Erwin, J., and H. A. Andrews. "State of Part-Time Faculty Services at Community Colleges in a Nineteen-State Region." *Community College Journal of Research and Practice* 17, no. 6 (1993):555–562.

Evans, G., G. Hagedorn, and M. Woods. "Part-Time Faculty—Poison or Cure for Higher Education's Ills?" Proceedings of the National Conference on Professional Development of Part-Time Occupational Technical Faculty, Scottsdale, AZ (1990):91–95.

"Fall Staff in Postsecondary Institutions, 1997." National Center for Education Statistics, Document NCES 2000-164.

Farrell, T .J. "How to Kill Higher Education." *Academe* 78, no. 6 (1992):30–33.

Fogg, Piper. "Court Upholds Ruling That Allows Adjuncts at Keene State College to Unionize." *Chronicle of Higher Education*, April 22, 2002. http://chronicle.com/daily/2002/04/2002042202n.htm.

Foster, D., and E. Foster. "It's a Buyer's Market: 'Disposable Professors,' Grade Inflation and Other Problems." *Academe* 84, no. 1 (1998):28–35.

Fulton, Richard D. "The Plight of Part-Timers in Higher Education: Some Ruminations and Suggestions." *Change* 32 (May/June 2000):38–43.

Gadberry, Joseph L., and Helen Burnstad. "One Faculty: Hiring Practices and Orientation." In *Adjunct Faculty in Community Colleges*, ed. Desna L. Wallin, 75–95. Bolton, MA: Anker (2005).

Gappa, J. M. "Employing Part-Time Faculty: Thoughtful Approaches to Continuing Problems." *AAHE Bulletin* 37, no. 2 (1984):3–7.

Gappa, J., and D. Leslie. "Education's New Academic Work Force." *Planning for Higher Education* 22 (1994):1–6.

German, Kathleen M. "Part-time Faculty: Identifying the Trends and Challenges." *Journal of the Association for Communication Administration* 3 (1996):231–241.

Gottfried, Bradley M. "Part-time Faculty in Community Colleges: Esteemed Contributors or Invisible Entities." *Michigan Community College Journal: Research and Practice* 1, no. 2 (1995):29–38.

Gravois, John. Adjunct Professors Discuss Labor Issues and College "Corporatization" at Biennial Conference. *The Chronicle of Higher Education*, August 2006.

Grusin, E., and B. Reed. "The Role of Part-Time Faculty in the Quality of Instruction." *Journalism Educator* (1994):15–26.

Hirsch, E. "The Plight of Part-Time Faculty." *AAUPC News* (December 1, 1993):3–4.

Huffman, John. "Adjuncts and Their Din of Inequities: Transforming Complaints Into Action and Results." Paper presented at the Forum of the Midwest Modern Languages Association, Chicago, IL, November 7, 1997.

Jacoby, D. "Effects of Part-Time Faculty Employment on Community College Graduation Rates." *Journal of Higher Education*, 77(6), 2006, 1081–1103.

Jonas, Peter M., and Don Weimer. "Do Part-Time Faculty Fully Understand the Values of an Institution? If Not, What Can Be Done About It?" Paper presented at the 37th Annual Meeting of the Association for Institutional Research, Orlando, FL, May 18–21, 1997.

Kean, P. "Temps Perdus." *Lingua Franca* (March 1994):49–53.

Kelly, D. K. "Part-Time Faculty in the Community College: A Study of Their Qualifications, Frustrations, and Involvement." Paper presented at the 31st Annual Forum of the Association for Institutional Research, San Francisco, CA, May 1991.

Kimmelman, M. "Quality Assurance for Part-Time Faculty." *Business Education Forum* 46 (1992):5–6.

Krier, D., and W. G. Staples. "Seen but Unseen: Part-Time Faculty and Institutional Surveillance and Control." *American Sociologist* 24, no. 3–4 (1993):119–134.

Leatherman, C. "Heavy Reliance on Low-Paid Lecturers Said to Produce 'Faceless Departments.'" *Chronicle of Higher Education*, March 28, 1997, sec. A, pp. 12–13.

Lesko, P. D. "What Scholarly Associations Should Do to Stop the Exploitation of Adjuncts." *Chronicle of Higher Education*, December 15, 1995, sec. B, p. 3.

Leslie, D. "Part-Time, Adjunct, and Temporary Faculty: The New Majority?" Report of the Sloan Conference on Part-Time and Adjunct Faculty, Arlington, VA, December 2–3, 1997.

Leslie, D., and J. Gappa. "Education's New Work Force." *Planning for Higher Education* 22 (1994):1–6.

Leslie, D., and J. Gappa. "The Part-Time Faculty Advantage." *Metropolitan Universities* 6, no. 2 (1995):91–102.

Levite, K. H. "Part-Time Educators: More Valuable Than Their Paychecks Indicate." *OATYC Journal* 15 (1990):33–34.

Longmate, Jack, and Frank Cosco. 2002. "Part-Time Instructors Deserve Equal Pay for Equal Work." *Chronicle of Higher Education*, May 3, 2002. http://chronicle.com/weekly/v48/i34/34b01401.htm.

Lowther, M. A., J. S. Stark, M. L. Genthon, and R. J. Bentley. "Comparing Introductory Course Planning Among Full-Time and Part-Time Faculty." *Research in Higher Education* 31, no. 6 (1990):495–517.

Lyons, Richard E. "A Strategic Model for Integrating Adjunct Faculty into the College Culture." In *Adjunct Faculty in Community Colleges*, ed. Desna L. Wallin, 127–142. Bolton, MA: Anker, 2005.

McArthur, Ronald C. "A Comparison of Grading Patterns Between Full- and Part-Time Humanities Faculty: A Preliminary Study." *Community College Review* 27 (winter 1999):65–76.

McGuire, J. "Part-Time Faculty: Partners in Excellence." *Leadership Abstracts* 6, no. 6 (1993):2–3.

McKenna, B. "Off the Tenure Track." *On Campus* (May 1997):6–7, 15.

Monroe, Craig, and Sarah Denman. "Assimilating Adjunct Faculty: Problems and Opportunities." *ACA Bulletin* 77 (August 1991):56–62.

Moore, Linda B. "Citizen Responsibility by and for Part-Time Faculty." Paper presented at the 48th Annual Meeting of the Conference on College Composition and Communication, Phoenix, AZ, March 12–15, 1997.

Moser, Richard. "The New Academic Labor System, Corporatization and the Renewal of Academic Citizenship." Washington, DC: American Association of University Professors (2001).

Nance, G., and R. Culberhouse. "The Hidden Costs of Part-Time Faculty." *Planning for Higher Education* 20 (1991):30–38.

Naquin, Debbie. "The Increasing Reliance on Part-Time Faculty: A Problem with Legal Implications." *Inquiry* 6, no. 1 (2001):34–42.

National Center for Education Statistics. *Changes in Staff Distribution and Salaries of Full-Time Employees in Postsecondary Institutions: Fall 1993–2003.* Washington, DC: Author, 2006.

National Education Association. "Part-Time Temporary & Nontenure Track Faculty Appointments." (1987). Washington, DC: Author.

Nicol, David J. "Preparation and Support of Part-Time Teachers in Higher Education." *Teacher Development* 4, no. 1 (2000):115–129.

Pankin, R. M., and C. Weiss. "Working Part-Time Full-Time." *AAUPC News* (February 14, 1994):2, 5–6.

Parsons, Michael H. "How the Other 2/3 Live: Institutional Initiative for Part-Time

Faculty Assimilation in America's 2-Year Colleges." Paper presented at the 78th Annual Convention of the American Association of Community Colleges, Miami, FL, April 24, 1998.

Rajgopal, I., and W. D. Farr. "Mediative Roles for Management: Collective Bargaining with Part-Time Faculty." *Journal for Higher Education Management* 8, no. 2 (1993):67–81.

Reichard, G. W. "Part-Time Faculty in Research Universities: Problems and Prospects." *Academe* 84, no. 1 (1998):40–43.

Rhoades, G. "Reorganizing the Faculty Workforce for Flexibility." *Journal of Higher Education* 67, no. 6 (Fall 996):626–659.

Roueche, J. E., and S. D. Roueche. "Identifying the Strangers: Exploring Part-Time Faculty Integration in American Community Colleges." *Community College Review* 23 (1996):33–48.

Schneider, Alison. "More Professors Are Working Part-Time, and More Teach at 2-Year Colleges." *Chronicle of Higher Education*, March 13, 1998, sec. A, p. 15.

Schuet, P. "Instructional Practices of Part-Time and Full-Time Faculty." In *New Directions for Community Colleges* no. 118. *Community College Faculty: Characteristics, Practices, and Challenges*, ed. C. L. Outcalt, 39–46. San Francisco: Jossey-Bass, 2002.

Schuster, J. H. "Reconfiguring the Professoriate: An Overview." *Academe* 84, no. 1 (1998):48–53.

Scott, John. "Supporting Adjunct Faculty Members: Affordable Options." *Michigan Community College Journal: Research & Practice* 3 (Fall 1997):31–42.

Selvadurai, Ranjani H. "Advantages and Disadvantages of Hiring Part-Time Faculty in Higher Education." *Community Review* 10, no. 1–2 (1990):35–36.

Smallwood, Scott. "Adjuncts at New York U. Have 3 Choices in Union Vote." *Chronicle of Higher Education*, April 22, 2002. http://chronicle.com/daily/2002/04/2002042203n.htm.

Smith, Milton L. "The Adjunct/Full-Time Faculty Ratio." *New Directions for Community Colleges* 18, no. 1 (1990):71–82.

Sommer, B. "Recognizing Academe's Other Faculty." *Planning for Higher Education* 22 (1994):7–10.

Sonner, Brenda S. "A is for 'Adjuncts': Examining Grade Inflation in Higher Education." *Journal of Education for Business* 76, no. 1 (2000):5–8.

Statement from the Conference on the Growing Use of Part-Time and Adjunct Faculty. *Academe* 84, no. 1 (1998):54–60.

Styne, M. "Those Unfamiliar Names and Faces: The Hiring, Management, and Evaluation of Part-Time Faculty." *Teaching English in the Two-Year College* 24, no. 1 (1997):50–55.

Thompson, K. "Recognizing Mutual Interests." *Academe* 78, no. 6 (1992):22–26.

Tobin, Elizabeth H. "Treating Part-Time Faculty Equitably: One College's Solutions." *Peer Review* 5, no. 1 (2002):22–24.

Tuckman, H. P., J. Caldwell, and W. Vogler. "Part-Timers and the Academic Labor Market of the Eighties." *The American Sociologist* 13, no. 4 (1978):184–195.

Tyree, Larry W., Pat Grunder, and April O'Connell. "Mending the Rift Between Full Time and Part Time Faculty." *Community College Journal* 70 (Feb–March 2000):24–28.

U.S. Department of Education, National Center for Education Statistics. "Background Characteristics, Work Activities, and Compensation of Faculty and Instructional Staff in Postsecondary Institutions: Fall 1998." (Report NCES 2001–152) Washington DC: Author.

Wallin, D. L. "Valuing Professional Colleagues: Adjunct Faculty in Community and Technical Colleges." *Community College Journal of Research and Practice* 28 (2004):1–19.

Wilson, Robin. "Proportion of Part-Time Faculty Members Leveled Off from 1992 to 1998, Data Show." *Chronicle of Higher Education*, May 4, 2001. http://chronicle.com/weekly/v47/i34/34a01400i.htm.

Wilson, Robin. 1996. "Scholars Off the Tenure Track Wonder If They'll Ever Get On."

Chronicle of Higher Education, June 14, 1996. http://chronicle.com.

Ziegler, Carol A., and Marianne Reiff. "Adjunct Mentoring, a Vital Responsibility in a Changing Educational Climate: The Lesley University Adjunct Mentoring Program," *Mentoring & Tutoring* 14, no. 2 (May 2006):247–269.

APPENDICES

Recommended Practices

Source: Gappa and Leslie (1993), pp. 234–276.

√ Indicates discussion of this practice is included in this book

	1	Develop goals for the use of part-time faculty that are based on the educational mission of the college or university.
	2	Include the use of part-time faculty in the overall faculty staffing plan.
	3	Consult part-time faculty during the development of faculty staffing plan.
	4	Assign responsibility, delegate authority, develop policies and guidelines, and review and monitor adherence to policy.
	5	Systematically and routinely gather and use accurate and timely data on part-time faculty for decision-making purposes.
	6	Periodically survey part-time faculty for additional information about their perceptions of the conditions under which they work, their satisfaction with their employment, and other concerns or interests.
	7	Assess the benefits and short- and long-term costs of employing part-time faculty.
	8	Review and evaluate the faculty staffing plan on a regular basis.
	9	Establish a campuswide representative body to give advice on part-time faculty employment policies.
√	10	Publish part-time faculty employment policies in the faculty manual and distribute them to all department chairs and faculty, especially the part-time faculty.
√	11	Make department chairs responsible for implementing part-time faculty employment policies consistently.
√	12	Offer a range of employment options for part-time faculty.
	13	Provide for part-time tenure.
√	14	Provide security and due-process rights for part-timers with seniority and records of effective performance.
√	15	Appoint continuing part-time faculty for more extended periods.
√	16	Establish career tracks that provide rewards and incentives for long-term service and/or high achievement.

(continues)

√ 17	Identify qualifications for part-time faculty that are legitimately related to the job requirements.
√ 18	Recruit, select, and hire part-time faculty proactively.
19	Diversify the part-time faculty pool through affirmative action.
√ 20	Provide timely and early notification of appointments to part-time positions.
√ 21	Develop a salary scale for part-time faculty.
√ 22	Ensure consistency of compensation practices for part-timers within departments and institutions.
√ 23	Set standards for progression through the salary scale.
√ 24	Provide benefits to continuing part-time faculty.
√ 25	Develop objective performance criteria and procedures for evaluating part-time faculty and use the results as the basis for decisions about reappointment.
√ 26	Provide support services to part-time faculty.
√ 27	Communicate the message that part-time faculty are important to the institution.
√ 28	Give department chairs responsibility and incentives to supervise part-time faculty.
29	Orient department chairs to good supervisory practice.
30	Invite part-time faculty to share their perceptions of effective supervisory practice at department chair training sessions.
√ 31	Use teams of experienced faculty (full- and part-time) to develop new faculty members' teaching skills.
√ 32	Provide faculty mentors to inexperienced part-time faculty.
√ 33	Engage full- and part-time faculty in course coordination.
√ 34	Involve part-time faculty in the assessment of student learning.
√ 35	Appoint part-time faculty to committees.
√ 36	Involve part-time faculty in informal talks.
√ 37	Invite part-time faculty to social events.
√ 38	Publicly recognize part-time faculty for their achievements and contributions.

√ 39	Orient part-time faculty to the institution and to the expectations the institution has for them.
√ 40	Conduct frequent workshops on good teaching practices.
√ 41	Provide in-service professional development opportunities for part-time faculty.
√ 42	Provide incentive for good performance.
√ 43	Use teaching evaluations to help part-time faculty improve.

Gappa, Judith M., and Leslie, David W. (1993). *The Invisible Faculty: Improving the Status of Part-Timers in High Education*. San Francisco: Jossey-Bass Inc.

Sample Practices from Institutions across the Country

Over the past few years many institutions of all types—community and junior colleges, four-year colleges, research universities, and distance education programs—have instituted policies and practices that address the needs of part-time faculty. Many of these practices are in line with the suggestions in this volume. Typically, information about part-time faculty policies and practices is published in institutional handbooks for part-time faculty. Some of these are separate from full-time faculty's handbooks, others are sections within the full-time faculty's handbook. Many of these handbooks are available on the World Wide Web and are relatively easy to access through institutional Web sites. Access is also available through Google, primarily through two searches: "part-time faculty handbooks" and "adjunct faculty handbooks."

The institutions listed below have adopted some part-time faculty policies and practices. They are not listed here as "best practices" since their efficacy has neither been studied nor demonstrated. Rather, these are examples of institutional thinking meant to introduce the reader to some concrete samples of practice.

- Bates College, Lewiston, Maine
- Boston College, Chestnut Hill, Massachusetts
- Brookhaven College, Dallas, Texas
- Central Oregon Community College, Bend
- College of DuPage, Glen Ellyn, Illinois
- Community College of Vermont—Multiple locations around the state
- Eastern Kentucky University, Richmond
- Indian River Community College, Ft. Pierce, Florida
- Jackson Community College, Jackson, Michigan

- Johnson County Community College, Overland Park, Kansas
- Lakeland Community College, Kirtland, Ohio
- Lesley University, Cambridge, Massachusetts
- Loras College, Dubuque, Iowa
- Nevada State System of Higher Education
- Temple University, Philadelphia, Pennsylvania
- University of Arkansas, Little Rock
- Valencia Community College, Orlando, Florida
- Williams College, Williamstown, Massachusetts

doctoral dissertations: on part-time faculty,
106–14
duplication services, 55

Elman, Sandra E., 16
e-mail: access to, 19, 37, 55
evaluation: peer, 73–74; performance, 52
experience-based learning: opportunities for,
88–90

Faculty Club, 20, 39
Faculty Senate: and achievement awards, 41;
representation on, 35
feedback: two-minute, 75–76
fellowships: to part-time faculty, 93
field applications, 97; projects on, 89
field trips, 88–89
FIFSE. *See* Fund for the Improvement of
Postsecondary Education
financial issues, 25–27
forums: participation in, 35
4faculty, 69
Fulbright Scholar Program, 95
Fund for the Improvement of Postsecondary
Education (FIPSE), 16

grading standards: setting, participation in,
66–67
grants: to part-time faculty, 93
grievance policies, 36
group benefits, 28–29
Guggenheim fellowships, 93, 95

handbooks, 32–34
health care: access to, 28
hiring, 50; notice of, 41

ID cards, 38
information: access to, 51, 95–97
information literacy: workshops on, 68
institution: connection to, 13–43; organizational climate and culture of, 15; orientation to, 29–32; participation in life of,
34–36, 85–86
internships, 89

job fairs, 22
John Simon Guggenheim Memorial Foundation, 93, 95
journal: reflective, 74

knowledge: shared, 98–99

large classes: support for, 85
learning: experience-based, opportunities
for, 88–90; problem-based, 89; scholarship of, 94–95; service, 88
learning development activities: participation
in, 64–67
learning environment, 79–90
Library of Congress, 96
library privileges, 19, 38–39
low-cost benefits, 28

mail distribution, 55
materials: duplication of, 55; review of, 74;
selection of, 51
meetings: departmental, 51–52
Mellon Post-doctoral Fellowships, 96
mentor(s): roles of, 58–59; selection of, 57
mentoring, 55–59; duration of, 57; format of,
58; of students, 86–88
mentoring program: goals of, 56; origination
and structure of, 56–57
micro-teaching, 74
motivations: of part-time faculty, 7

names: in print, 84
National Endowment for the Arts, 96
National Endowment for the Humanities,
96
National Humanities Center, 96
National Science Foundation, 96
needs determination, 21–22
Nelson, Cary, 9
no-cost benefits, 28
notice of hiring, 41

observation: classroom, 74
office hours: and pay, 26
office space, 54–55
Online Faculty Teaching Excellence Network (OFTEN), 69